HOW I RESIST

HOW I RESIST

ACTIVISM AND HOPE FOR A NEW GENERATION

— EDITED BY —

MAUREEN JOHNSON

WEDNESDAY BOOKS
NEW YORK

HOW I RESIST. Copyright © 2018 by Maureen Johnson. All rights reserved. Printed in the United States of America. For information, address St. Martin's Press, 175 Fifth Avenue, New York, N.Y. 10010.

www.wednesdaybooks.com
www.stmartins.com

Designed by Anna Gorovoy

Illustrations by Jonathan Bush; KC Green illustration by KC Green

Illustrations based on images as follows: Jacqueline Woodson by Marty Umans Photography; Ali Stroker by Ali Stroker; Alex Gino by Alex Gino; Carolyn DeWitt by Carolyn DeWitt; Rebecca Roanhorse by Stephen Lang; Dana Schwartz by Dana Schwartz; Daniel J. Watts by Travis Magee; Lauren Duca by Damon Scheleur; Hebh Jamal by Hebh Jamal; Javier Muñoz by Javier Muñoz; Jeffrey Rowland by Holly R. Rowland; Jennifer Weiner by Jennifer Weiner; Jodi Picoult by Splash News/Alamy Stock Photo; John Paul Brammer by Gregor Hochmuth on Behalf of Dreams, Media, Inc.; Jonny Sun by Christopher Sun; Junauda Petrus by Sarah White; Karuna Riazi by Linda Rosier; Libba Bray by Libba Bray; Malinda Lo by Malinda Lo; Maya Rupert by Maya Rupert; Sabaa Tahir by Christophe Testi; Shaina Taub by Matt Gehring; Jason Reynolds by ZUMA Press, Inc./Alamy Stock Photo; Jesse Tyler Ferguson and Justin Mikita by Emma McIntyre/Getty Images; Dan Sinker by Dan Sinker; Rosie O'Donnell by Walter McBride/Getty Images; Kate Linnea Welsh by Kate Linnea Welsh

The Library of Congress Cataloging-in-Publication Data is available upon request.

ISBN 978-1-250-16836-8 (trade paperback)
ISBN 978-1-250-16837-5 (ebook)

Our books may be purchased in bulk for promotional, educational, or business use. Please contact your local bookseller or the Macmillan Corporate and Premium Sales Department at 1-800-221-7945, extension 5442, or by email at MacmillanSpecialMarkets@macmillan.com.

First Edition: May 2018

10 9 8 7

COPYRIGHT ACKNOWLEDGMENTS

"Could We Please Give the Police Departments to the Grandmothers?" Copyright © 2018 by Junauda Petrus.

"Keep Doing What You're Doing." Copyright © 2018 by Malinda Lo.

"Why We ALL Need to Be Activists Right Now." Copyright © 2017 by Lauren Duca. This was originally published in *Teen Vogue* in February 2017.

"Thoughts on Resistance." Copyright © 2018 by Rebecca Roanhorse.

"5 Things Teens Can Do to Engage in Politics Before Turning 18." Copyright © 2018 by Carolyn DeWitt.

Hebh Jamal Essay. Copyright © 2018 by Hebh Jamal.

"The Lucky Ones." Copyright © 2018 by Jennifer Weiner.

"Letter to a Sensitive Brown Queer." Copyright © 2018 by John Paul Brammer.

[vi] COPYRIGHT ACKNOWLEDGMENTS

"The Clap Back." Copyright © 2018 by Daniel J. Watts.

"When." Copyright © 2018 by Shaina Taub.

"Part of the Problem." Copyright © 2018 by KC Green.

"Making Stuff That Matters." Copyright © 2018 by Dan Sinker.

"I, Wonder: Imagining a Black Wonder Woman." Copyright © 2017 by Maya Rupert. This was originally published in *The Atlantic* in May 2017.

"Rosie O'Donnell's Five Resistance Steps." Copyright © 2018 by Rosie O'Donnell.

"An Announcement From Muffy Higginbottom, President of Delta Sigma Tau Sorority Resistance Committee." Copyright © 2018 by Martha E. Bray.

"Media-Consciousness as Part of Resistance!" Copyright © 2018 by Jonny Sun.

Jodi Picoult Essay. Copyright © 2018 by Jodi Picoult.

"Three Easy Steps to Contact Your Reps." Copyright © 2018 by Kate Linnea Welsh.

Alex Gino Essay. Copyright © 2018 by Alex Gino.

Sabaa Tahir Poem. Copyright © 2018 by Sabaa Tahir.

COPYRIGHT ACKNOWLEDGMENTS [vii]

"The Jewish We." Copyright © 2018 by Dana Schwartz.

Jeffrey Rowland Cartoon. Copyright © 2018 by Jeffrey Rowland.

"Refilling the Well." Copyright © 2018 by Karuna Riazi.

This book is for all of you out there calling, marching, working, running for office, working on campaigns, working for agencies, talking to friends and relatives, posting, and keeping the conversation going.

For those of you just being yourselves in places and in situations where being yourself isn't easy.

For your multitudinous acts of resistance, for your courage, for getting up and doing it again each day . . . for your hope in the future. Thank you.

CONTENTS

Acknowledgments [xv]

What is Resistance? [1]

"Could We Please Give the Police Departments to the Grandmothers?"
Junauda Petrus [3]

Interview
Dylan Marron [9]

"Keep Doing What You're Doing"
Malinda Lo [17]

"Why We ALL Need to Be Activists Right Now"
Lauren Duca [23]

"Thoughts on Resistance"
Rebecca Roanhorse [29]

Interview
Jason Reynolds [33]

[xii] CONTENTS

"5 Things Teens Can Do to Engage in Politics Before Turning 18"
Carolyn DeWitt   [41]

Essay
Hebh Jamal   [45]

Interview
Javier Muñoz   [51]

"The Lucky Ones"
Jennifer Weiner   [61]

"Letter to a Sensitive Brown Queer"
John Paul Brammer   [69]

"The Clap Back"
Daniel J. Watts   [75]

Interview
Ali Stroker   [83]

"When"
Shaina Taub   [89]

"Part of the Problem"
KC Green   [105]

"Making Stuff That Matters"
Dan Sinker   [109]

CONTENTS [xiii]

"I, Wonder: Imagining a Black Wonder Woman"
Maya Rupert [115]

"Rosie O'Donnell's Five Resistance Steps"
Rosie O'Donnell [123]

Interview
Jacqueline Woodson [127]

"An Announcement From Muffy Higginbottom, President of Delta Sigma Tau Sorority Resistance Committee"
Libba Bray [133]

"Media-Consciousness as Part of Resistance!"
Jonny Sun [141]

Essay
Jodi Picoult [153]

"Three Easy Steps to Contact Your Reps"
Kate Linnea Welsh [159]

Essay
Alex Gino [163]

Interview
Justin Mikita and Jesse Tyler Ferguson [169]

Poem
Sabaa Tahir [177]

[xiv] CONTENTS

"The Jewish We"
Dana Schwartz   [181]

Cartoon
Jeffrey Rowland   [187]

"Refilling the Well"
Karuna Riazi   [191]

The Bigness Trap   [197]

The Beginner's Guide to Books on Resistance   [199]

ACKNOWLEDGMENTS

To the incredible Kate Welsh, who kept every spreadsheet, read every email, checked every box, edited, responded, tracked, and generally sweated every detail so that each one of these amazing contributions made it into the book. Without her, there would be no book. Thank you to Sara and everyone at St. Martin's/Wednesday for giving this book a place to call home. To my agent, Kate Schafer Testerman, who is all things to me. To Cheryl Klein, who helped curate the book list. To my friend Dan Sinker, who encouraged me to make a podcast about resistance (it's called *Says Who*—come join us!) and who taught me how to stop worrying and MAKE. And to the incredible contributors who gave so freely of themselves for this book. Thank you all.

HOW I RESIST

WHAT IS RESISTANCE?

When I told people I was working on a resistance guide for teens, occasionally someone would ask me, "Why? They can't vote."

I would just shake my head. Adults are so dumb sometimes. We forget that we were all teens—NO ONE HAS SKIPPED THIS STEP. We spent most of our time in school learning stuff like history, social studies, public speaking, composition. You know, stuff to make us better members of society. Adults forget that we knew stuff back then and had opinions and that there is no magic transformation that occurs when the clock ticks you over from age seventeen to eighteen. You, my teenage friends, are voters-in-training, the same as adults. Adults forget that we are *all* voters-in-training. The learning process never stops. We need to look to our younger citizens and non-citizens because you're the ones coming at subjects for the first time; your perspectives, as a result, are fresh and passionate. You practice learning every day. You know how the Internet works. You have not developed the often rigid ways of thinking that plague adults.

In short, you are often better at activism.

Tragically, it took the Marjory Stoneman Douglas High School shooting in Parkland, Florida, to make this point clear to everyone. When the students rose and made the Never Again movement, when you debated senators in a televised town hall a week later, when you led students across

[2] MAUREEN JOHNSON

the country to take action on gun control . . . everyone knew that you had changed the program.

This book came about because I had that strange, sucking feeling in my soul after the 2016 election—the one that made me (and almost everyone I know) ask, "But what can I do? WHAT CAN I DO?" The question haunted me day and night. "I only know how to make books," I said to myself.

So I decided to do that.

Here is a book about resistance for teens. (And anyone else who wants to read this book. ALL ARE WELCOME HERE. We are all in training, remember.)

On the most basic level, resistance means not accepting things the way they are. It means asking questions about how things get done, about how society, laws, and cultural norms have come to be. It can also mean actively taking part in the political process—going to marches, working for campaigns, posting, debating, creating. . . .

It can mean a lot of things.

In these pages you're going to find different types of materials. There are essays. There are poems. There are songs. There are cartoons. There are lists. There are interviews. There are sample letters to help you contact your representatives. There is information about specific actions people under eighteen can take. There is advice on how to step out of your comfort zone and make something.

Read this book in any order you want—start at the beginning and read it through, or open at random. Whatever speaks to you . . . wonderful. It's not a prescription; it's a way to get you going. Your acts of resistance will vary. Your ways of approaching issues will differ. Good. That's the way it should be. Resistance isn't a set of steps—it is an ecosystem in which all the different creations live and help one another grow.

These are hard times, but also times of great opportunity. So come on in and let's get to it!

Junauda Petrus is a creative activist, writer, playwright, screenwriter, and multidimensional performance artist who is Minneapolis-born, of West Indian descent, and African-sourced. She is the cofounder with Erin Sharkey of Free Black Dirt, an experimental arts production company. She is currently writing and directing Sweetness of Wild, *a web series themed around Blackness, queerness, biking, resistance, love, and coming of age in Minneapolis. Her work centers around wildness, Afrofuturism, ancestral healing, sweetness, spectacle, and shimmer. Her first YA novel,* Mable & Audre's Existential Transcendental Journey Through Black Universe, *debuts in 2019 from Dutton Children's Books. Follow her on Twitter @junaundaalma and Instagram @Junauda.*

COULD WE PLEASE GIVE THE POLICE DEPARTMENTS TO THE GRANDMOTHERS?

Could we please give the police departments to the grandmothers? Give them the salaries and the pensions and the city vehicles, but make them a fleet of vintage Corvettes, Jaguars, and Cadillacs, with white leather interior. Diamond in the back, sunroof top, and digging the scene with the gangsta lean.

Let the cars be badass!

You would hear the old-school jams from Patti LaBelle, Anita Baker, and Al Green. You would hear Sweet Honey in the Rock harmonizing on "Ella's Song": *We who believe in freedom cannot rest . . .* bumping out the speakers.

And they got the booming system.

If you're up to mischief, they will pick you up swiftly in their sweet ride and look at you until you catch shame and look down at your lap. She asks you if you are hungry and you say yes and of course you are. She's got a crown of dreadlocks and on the dashboard you see brown faces like yours, shea buttered and loved up.

And there are no precincts.

Just love temples that got spaces to meditate and eat delicious food. Mangoes, blueberries, nectarines, cornbread, peas and rice, fried plantain, fufu, yams, greens, okra, pecan pie, salad, and lemonade.

[6] MAUREEN JOHNSON

Things that make your mouth water and soul arrive.

All the hungry bellies know warmth, all the children expect love. The grandmas help you with homework, practice yoga with you, and teach you how to make jambalaya and coconut cake. From scratch.

When you're sleepy she will start humming and rub your back while you drift off. A song that she used to have the record of when she was your age. She remembers how it felt to be you and be young and not know the world that good. Grandma is a sacred child herself, who just circled the sun enough times into the ripeness of her cronehood.

She wants your life to be sweeter.

When you are wildin' out because your heart is broke or you don't have what you need, the grandmas take your hand and lead you to their gardens. You can lay down amongst the flowers. Her grasses, roses, dahlias, irises, lilies, collards, kale, eggplants, blackberries. She wants you to know that you are safe and protected, universal limitless, sacred, sensual, divine, and free.

Grandma is the original warrior, wild since birth, comfortable in loving fiercely. She has fought so that you don't have to, not in the same ways at least.

So give the police departments to the grandmas, they are fearless, classy, and actualized. Blossomed from love. They wear what they want and say what they please.

Believe that.

There wouldn't be noise citations when the grandmas ride through our streets, blasting Stevie Wonder, Nina Simone, Marvin Gaye, Alice Coltrane, Jimi Hendrix, KRS-One. All that good music. The kids gonna hula hoop to it and sell her lemonade made from heirloom pink lemons and maple syrup. The car is solar powered and carbon footprint–free, the grandmas designed the technology themselves.

At night they park the cars in a circle so all can sit in them with the sun-

HOW I RESIST [7]

roofs open and look at the stars, talk about astrological signs, what to plant tomorrow based on the moon's mood, and help you memorize Audre Lorde and James Baldwin quotes. She always looks you in the eye and acknowledges the light in you with no hesitation or fear. And Grandma loves you fiercely forever.

She sees the pain in our bravado, the confusion in our anger, the depth behind our coldness. Grandma knows what oppression has done to our souls and is gonna change it one love temple at a time. She has no fear.

DYLAN MARRON

Dylan Marron is a writer, performer, and videomaker whose work blends social justice activism and entertainment. He voices Carlos on Welcome to Night Vale and created Every Single Word, *a video series that edits down popular films to only feature the words spoken by people of color.* Dylan created, hosted, and produced interview shows like Sitting in Bathrooms with Trans People *and* Shutting Down Bullsh*t, *as well as his signature* Unboxing *series. For* Conversations with People Who Hate Me, *his popular podcast, he calls up folks who have said negative or hateful things about him on the internet. Follow him on Twitter @dylanmarron.*

Dylan, you're known for many things, like playing Carlos on *Welcome to Night Vale*, *Every Single Word*, *Sitting in Bathrooms with Trans People*, and now *Conversations with People Who Hate Me*. I'd like to start with the last one. What made you decide to make *Conversations with People Who Hate Me*?

DYLAN: I feel like the through line that runs through most of my work is that I take what hurts me, sit with it, and then try and package it in an accessible way. So something like *Every Single Word* came from being told over and over again by talent agents that I was talented enough to deserve work but unlikely to get it. To explain this, they would say that I was too "specific," a euphemism that the industry likes to throw around when you don't fit into a box of the preapproved "types." At the intersection of two different identities—brown and queer—this posed too much specificity, apparently, for the entertainment industry to handle.

"Specific"? I'm kind of staggered by the implications of this term.

DYLAN: Oh yes. It's horrible. Ultimately the word hints at the larger idea that, as a member of a marginalized group—and, God forbid, two—you are

[12] MAUREEN JOHNSON

not afforded the privilege of nuance in media. You're either "the Latino guy" or "the gay one." It's too much to ask to be just "you."

So I made the *Every Single Word* series as a way to talk about the lack of representation of people of color in film, but I wanted to present it in an accessible, empirical way that allowed people to consume it quickly yet it was an arrow to a larger problem.

Conversations with People Who Hate Me sprouted from a similar seed. Throughout my years of making publicly consumable digital work, I found that I was getting a lot of hateful comments and messages. These hate messages would ruin my day, sometimes my week. But once I got over the initial pain of the comments, I wanted to know who was writing them. Why were they writing them? What's their story? So, the seeds of the podcast were planted.

Do you have one conversation that really stands out to you?

DYLAN: I don't like to play favorites with my guests! But there are two that stick out to me. In the second episode I speak to a soon-to-be graduating high school senior named Josh. Online he called me a "moron" and "the reason this country was dividing itself." Yet on the phone I learned that he is a sweet, good kid who is more nuanced than his initial message might suggest. In our conversation he revealed that he, himself, was bullied throughout high school, which was something I faced as well. And it was interesting because the kind of speech that was flung at him in school was echoed in what he wrote to me. And this is so human: when you're being hurt by someone you often hurt someone else. I know that's true for me, too. When I was in high school and bullied, I would often be a jerk to my

HOW I RESIST [13]

parents, but it was only because I felt so tiny in high school and that was my release.

What has been your main takeaway so far?

DYLAN: I think it's what I turned into my sign-off line. "Remember, there's a human on the other side of the screen." Because that goes both ways, you know? It's important to remember that when you're typing a comment to someone, but by the same token it's also important to remember when you're seeing the comment. Like, a human wrote that comment. What are they going through that they wanted to type that?

To be very clear, I don't mean to suggest that people who are the victims of online harassment should just empathize with their harasser, but I feel like I was afforded the privilege of a platform where I could take a step back and kind of survey the harassment I was getting and start considering who is on the other side.

But speaking to people who have said these kinds of things about you, that must be hard. How do you emotionally prepare for these kinds of conversations?

DYLAN: Hmm. I think if I thought about it that way I'd never do the project. I think the more emotionally draining part is receiving these messages and comments, sometimes at a pace that feels so overwhelming. The calls themselves are actually therapeutic to me, they help me humanize someone who was previously a stranger.

[14] MAUREEN JOHNSON

So the art itself is the emotional process for you?

DYLAN: One hundred percent.

Going back in time a bit, where did your activism life start? Because you've been making activist art for some time. Did you start as a teen?

DYLAN: I think the seeds of activism were planted for me in my childhood when I first learned I was brown, which is to say, when I first understood that people were classified by their race. For me that was when I was in the third grade and went to an open casting call for *Home Alone 3* and saw that the white kids were all moving on to the next round and the kids of color were immediately cut. Now, clearly, I didn't start protesting then but that was the first thing that tipped me off to the fact that an integral part of my identity, my brownness, was deemed as "other."

Similarly, when I started to realize I was queer, other seeds of activism were planted. Over time those seeds sprouted and, to continue the extended metaphor, they grew into a tree so big I couldn't ignore it.

I have to ask about Carlos. Carlos is a much-beloved character. I've seen the reactions of *Night Vale* fans when they watch Carlos and Cecil interact, and it's really moving. *Night Vale* itself, while entirely a story about a town in the desert in which all conspiracies are true, is also an act of activism. How do you feel about the fan reaction? What does it say to you?

DYLAN: I love the *Night Vale* fandom that I've gotten to meet over time and I love how immersed they are in the world of *Night Vale.* I definitely agree that *Night Vale* is an act of activism, but for some more behind-the-scenes reason. Joseph and Jeffrey are two artists who I have such immense respect for. They created this world before knowing what it was going to explode into. They did it because they loved it and didn't wait for anyone's permission to create. They just did it, and the world took notice. To me that's some radical activism.

Do you have any words of advice for teens who want to get into the political or activism process, but don't know where to start?

DYLAN: Yes. First, take your time. None of us come into the world fully aware of who we are or what cause we want to take up. Make mistakes, they are inevitable. And when you feel ready to get to that podium, literal or metaphorical, take what hurts you and try and make it hurt someone else less.

Malinda Lo is the author of several young adult novels, including A Line in the Dark. Her novel Ash, *a lesbian retelling of Cinderella, was a finalist for the William C. Morris YA Debut Award, the Andre Norton Award for YA Science Fiction and Fantasy, the Mythopoeic Fantasy Award, and was a Kirkus Best Book for Children and Teens. She has been a three-time finalist for the Lambda Literary Award. Malinda's nonfiction has been published by* The New York Times Book Review, NPR, HuffPost, The Toast, The Horn Book Magazine, *and* AfterEllen. *Her website is www.malindalo.com.*

KEEP DOING WHAT YOU'RE DOING

The day after the election in 2016, I called my parents. I had been in a daze all day, head fuzzy, bleary-eyed. I'd only gotten a few hours of sleep. When I woke up that morning, I had to grab my phone immediately to see if what I thought had happened the night before had really happened. Yes, Trump had been elected president.

It felt like an unnatural disaster. It felt like I had to check in with my parents, who live half a continent away from me. Some part of me wanted them to tell me it was going to be okay.

"It's terrible," my mom said, sounding as if she hadn't gotten much sleep either. She didn't say it was going to be okay. She told me she had given money to Hillary Clinton's campaign; it was the first time in her life she had given money to a politician.

"What are we supposed to do?" I asked, as if I were a kid again.

"Just keep doing what you're doing," my dad said. He also didn't say it was going to be okay.

This was not what I'd hoped for. My parents grew up in Communist China. They saw firsthand the way a government can lie to its people, the actions it can take to silence dissent, the shameless manner in which it can erase history. I thought my parents would tell me that America is not China, that democracy would prevail.

[20] MAUREEN JOHNSON

They didn't. They told me to just keep doing what I was doing.

I didn't understand what they meant. After the election I was glued to the news, watching Rachel Maddow, reading *The Washington Post,* listening to every politics podcast I could find. I was astonished—I was aghast—I was digging myself deeper and deeper into a hole of political despair.

For weeks after the election, I couldn't work. I had a short story due around that time, and I was dealing with the last edits on a novel, but when I sat down to work, the news continued to ceaselessly unspool in my mind. I'd tap out some words, but they were all wrong. I couldn't focus. It seemed pointless. I felt like I needed to protest, to call my representatives.

So I went to the Women's March. I called my representatives—even though they were Democrats. I gave money to the ACLU and tiny Democratic campaigns and Planned Parenthood. I spoke up online, adding my voice to the millions of other voices shouting in protest. Our voices together made a glorious roar, but as the months went by I began to wonder if it did anything besides prompt the Republicans to put in earplugs. It began to feel like screaming into a void.

I kept thinking about what my parents had said. It started to make sense.

Even before the Trump administration officially began, the news cycle had become an avalanche of shocking revelations, tantalizing leaks, and disturbing lies. Every day—sometimes every hour—a new twist blasted across the media. Paying attention to each new development made my head pound. And it was stripping me of my ability to do what I had worked my entire life to do: write fiction.

Writing fiction seemed incredibly frivolous in light of what was happening in our country. Sure, I was writing fiction about people that Trump would hate—queer teens and people of color—but I wasn't advocating for better health care, protesting the Muslim ban at airports, or running for office. Shouldn't I be doing more? Shouldn't I be doing something else? Those were the guilt-inducing questions cycling through my mind.

HOW I RESIST [21]

I had to shut off the news. I had to take some time away from the political trashfire that was burning out of control, and in the quiet space I cleared for myself, I remembered something important. Every human being here on earth has a specific purpose in life. That purpose might be running for office; it might be raising a child; it might be studying physics; it might be writing novels. Finding your purpose can be a difficult thing to do, but once you've found it, your job is to fulfill that purpose.

When my father was growing up in Communist China, he knew what his purpose in life should be. He wanted to study electronics and become an engineer. But in Communist China, you didn't get to follow your dreams unless the state decided you deserved it. My paternal grandfather had been labeled a Rightist—a political designation slapped on intellectuals who were believed to support capitalism—which meant he was criticized and persecuted under several Communist campaigns. It also meant my father inherited that label, and he wasn't allowed to pursue his interests. The Chinese government denied him admission to college; they sent him to the countryside to work in rice fields and build dams. And his father, who had been a professor of psychology, was no longer allowed to do his research.

The chaos of the Trump administration threatens all of us. It threatens us by stripping away our health care, destroying our environment, and discriminating against religious and ethnic minorities, women, and LGBTQ people. It threatens us by monopolizing our mental energy and draining our faith in democracy. All these threats can lead to despair, and despair robs us of our dreams and our purpose. Despair is the enemy of hope and progress.

We must fight against the threats of the Trump administration, and we must use all our tools to do that. Protests, phone calls, speaking out, voting—and making sure every citizen is able to cast their vote—are all necessary. But in the midst of seemingly endless bad news and despair-inducing decisions by spineless politicians, we must not lose sight of who we are as individuals. We must not let despair derail us from our purpose or our dreams.

All those years in China, my father kept doing what he was doing. Even though he was denied his hopes and dreams by the state, he taught himself electronics. When he immigrated to the United States, he put himself through night school, earning bachelor's and master's degrees in engineering. It took him decades, but he resisted the Chinese government's stifling of his dream.

Don't let Trump derail you. America is a country built on the premise—not always realized but always vital—that we should be free to pursue our dreams. Our freedom to do this—to create art, to be happy, to speak freely—is what makes this country the refuge my parents sought. Although America is far from perfect, it is the nation that enabled me to become the person I wanted to be: a writer.

So I'm going to keep doing what I'm doing. That is how we resist despair. That is how we resist.

Lauren Duca is an award-winning and -losing journalist known for her massively viral piece "Donald Trump Is Gaslighting America," a Fox News appearance opposite Tucker Carlson, and her Thigh-High Politics column for Teen Vogue. Since graduating from Fordham University in 2013, Lauren has won the Shorty Award for Best Journalist, been named one of Adweek's 15 Political Power Players, listed among Brooklyn Magazine's 100 cultural influencers, and honored with an Engendering Progress Award. Follow her on Twitter @laurenduca.

WHY WE ALL NEED TO BE ACTIVISTS RIGHT NOW

Way too many Americans think about politics in the way of the Olympics—like it's some big event that happens every few years, all but forgotten until the ad campaigns start up again. That's unacceptable from an intellectual perspective and also a practical one. America the idea wasn't magically complete because a bunch of white dudes in wigs wrote their names in fountain pen. The Declaration of Independence was always intended as a beginning, the formation of a dynamic entity that requires input, participation, and occasionally protest. The recent spike in political action has been painted as radical, but it should be closer to a core requirement for daily life in this country. Or, a bit less romantically, if America wants to be exceptional, we need to stop treating democracy like a self-cleaning litter box.

The glass-half-full reading of the election is that Trump's rise to power has awakened much of the public from a state of hibernation. Take a moment to relish in the invigorating statistics: in the five days following November 8, 2016, the American Civil Liberties Union collected $7 million from 120,000 donations (as compared to $28,000 from 354 donations over the same period in 2012, according to *The New York Times*). The day after the inauguration, statistical analysis site FiveThirtyEight estimated that more than three million people marched in more than three hundred U.S. cities in affirmation of not only women's rights, but a range of issues

[26] MAUREEN JOHNSON

united by the common theme of equality. Ever since the election, there has been a noticeable surge in efforts to contact representatives, and, oh, hey, those calls have been proven to work! (On a far smaller scale, more than fifty people sent me postcards announcing that they care about the release of Trump's tax returns—that's not insignificant.)

The resistance has a beating heart, and those numbers are the receipts to prove it. Now, to all the recently indoctrinated freedom fighters: welcome! There are many for whom none of this is new, and to them—especially the women of color who were marching long before January 21, 2017—newly activated activists owe gratitude, respect, and endurance. This can't be a fad. Let's not delude ourselves into thinking that picking up the phone, demonstrating, or donating is some funky thing we're trying for a couple of months, because those things are the starter kit for a politically active life. This has to be our routine, at least for the next four years and, if we all survive, well beyond it.

Each day brings a fresh crop of horrors, and the deluge is part of the strategy. The Trump administration is bombarding us with things to be devastated by, disseminating executive orders and disinformation with the rapidity of a malfunctioning strobe light. It's a drain-clogging effort aimed at lulling the country into a state of apathy by force of overload. When Trump and his surrogates pump falsehoods into the news cycle, the goal is not to convince the public of "alternative facts" but to make people throw up their hands in confusion and give up, thinking, "Who even knows what's true anymore?" Instead of worrying that they are attempting to distract and confuse us into oblivion, figure out a trustworthy media diet that makes sense for you, and stick to it. From there, be vigilant, and take action where necessary. I promise this will help manage that pesky feeling of inevitable doom. Take care of yourself, but also make a sustainable commitment to remaining productive. Angry energy without purpose will only turn into despair.

Pick something and then *do* something. That can be small, like a visit to the representative-contacting resource 5 Calls, or big, like bringing food and water to a protest. Trump's war on the truth takes aim at the foundation of all efforts to fight back. Staying informed is the bare minimum.

We're currently in a vortex of extended emergency. Every day feels like waking up from a perfectly boring dream to the realization that you've been sleeping on the cliffs of Mordor; giving this moment anything less than your all is the equivalent of hitting the snooze button. The Trump administration is waging a war on freedom, equality, and the truth. It's only slightly melodramatic to state that the very bedrock of democracy is under siege. Resisting the pull of Trump's chaotic brand of authoritarianism is going to be long, and hard, and more painful than you can possibly imagine. Unfortunately there is no viable alternative. Do not keep calm and carry on. This fraught moment calls for a paradigm shift in the way we think about participating in politics, and if the history of democracy has anything to say about it, the only American choice is to continue fighting.

Rebecca Roanhorse is an Ohkay Owingeh/Black writer of Indigenous futurisms and rez-based fantasy. She lives in northern New Mexico with her Navajo husband, daughter, and pug. Her science fantasy novel Trail of Lightning *is available summer 2018 and her children's book* Race to the Sun *from the Rick Riordan Presents imprint is coming in 2019.*

THOUGHTS ON RESISTANCE

Here's the truth.

Most days I'm too tired to resist.

Maybe you are, too.

Maybe after a day of work or school you feel lucky to just get home, stuff your face, and fall into bed. Maybe "resisting," whatever that means, feels like it's for other people, braver people, people out there doing things that you're not doing.

Maybe resisting is just asking too much.

When I was asked to participate in this anthology, I felt a mistake had been made. I'm not an activist. I'm not outspoken or well-known. I write science fiction and fantasy. I pretend for a living.

But then I remembered: I am an Indigenous woman. Every day I am alive is resistance.

Every day I am alive, I am resisting those who would reduce Native Americans to a footnote in a bad history book.

Every day I am alive, I am resisting those who say, "Oh, I thought all the Indians were dead."

Every day I am alive, I am resisting those who would reduce us to caricatures and mascots and Halloween costumes.

Every day I am alive, I am resisting those who want to deny our right to our languages, our land, our culture. I am resisting those who seek only to profit from Indigenous people—never to grieve with us, to laugh with us, to sit with us in protest. Or joy. Or silence.

Some of us have been resisting since 1492.

Last year, I saw Native nations and their allies rise up at Standing Rock and resist environmental injustice. They faced down water cannons in freezing temperatures and police dogs and rubber bullets. They were heroes, an inspiration.

But not all of us are cut out to be frontline pipeline warriors. And the good news is, we don't have to be.

If you're more like me, write. Imagine worlds with Indigenous people in them, whether your story takes place in New York or North Dakota. And imagine these people not just surviving, but thriving. Imagine them as doctors and fighter pilots and detectives and housewives raising children in the suburbs. If you write science fiction and fantasy, imagine Natives in space stations, Natives battling the Empire, Natives slaying dragons (of the North American variety, of course). Whatever you write, imagine worlds where brown and black girls challenge the status quo and stand up for themselves. Where they love themselves and each other. Where they get the happy-ever-after in the last act. Because imagining better worlds and writing them into being is my favorite kind of resistance of all.

What I know for a fact is that there is no one right way to resist. Some of us will march, some will call Congress, some will write stories, even when we're tired. And for some of us, our very lives are complex and beautiful acts of resistance.

Maybe yours is, too.

Maybe your resistance is to live. Live big and loud and joyously and fiercely. Live authentic to who you are. Refuse to be silent. Refuse to go away. Refuse stereotypes and limits.

Because you being you is the most powerful kind of resistance of all.

New York Times *bestselling author Jason Reynolds is the author of the critically acclaimed* When I Was the Greatest. *He is a National Book Award finalist, a Kirkus Prize winner, a Walter Dean Myers Award winner, an NAACP Image Award Winner, and the recipient of multiple Coretta Scott King Honors. His work includes the recently published* Long Way Down *and* Miles Morales: Spider-Man, *as well as* The Boy in the Black Suit, All American Boys *(cowritten with Brendan Kiely),* As Brave As You, *and the first two books in the Track series,* Ghost *and* Patina. *He is on faculty at Lesley University, for the Writing for Young People MFA Program.*

Does the word "resist" resonate with you?

JASON: Of course. I feel like, in essence, my entire existence is that of resistance, right? Like, who I am at my core is resistance. The way I look is resistance. Not just my skin—that's "born" resistance—but also the way I choose to look. My hair. My dress. It doesn't matter the space I'm in—I choose resistance.

When did you first feel called to resist?

JASON: I was sixteen. I'd gotten my first tattoo. (*Laughs.*) My father had taken me to get my first tattoo as a bonding experience—true story! He was covered in tattoos. He left when I was ten, but I grew up with a dude looking like I do today—except in the 1980s. A black man covered in tattoos, a gold chain, a badass dude in a way that black people weren't allowed to be at the time. He was badass in the way *white* guys saw. Rock 'n' roll . . . tattoos. A weird dissonance.

So when I turned sixteen he was like, "Yo, let's take you to get a tattoo." And I'm like, sweet—because I looked up and saw someone who was constantly resisting. I said, "Let's get the tattoo on my shoulder, so I can cover it up." And

[36] MAUREEN JOHNSON

he said, "Hell no, you're getting it on your forearm!" I'm sixteen! And the tattoo has praying hands and fire all around it, and it says "God free me." I remember coming back to school, and teachers being appalled at the fact that I had a visible tattoo at sixteen years old. And the questions they had for me, like: how are you expecting to get a job someday? And I was like: I'm not worried about getting a job. I'm going to be however I'm going to be. I was sixteen and if I wanted to do it I'd do it, and I didn't give a shit about who else cared.

In retrospect, are you glad you had that experience with your dad?

JASON: You know what, man? I am. Nowadays I have a little more wisdom, and I would have waited. You change so rapidly. I probably would have gotten a different kind of tattoo. But legitimately I'm pretty proud and happy about that moment, because even though my heart was broken and I felt abandoned by him, I still wanted to be him. "You're still Superman to me." So when he asked what I wanted for my birthday, and I said a tattoo, he said okay. And I remember him asking my mother: "Can I take Jason to get a tattoo for his birthday?" And she said okay! But when I came home and showed it to her, she's pissed! And she's pissed because even *she* had underestimated the will and certainty of her child. She thought I would get there and be like, *No* no no, I'm just joking. But my father took my word that we were going to do this. Then he said: what do *you* want? And he believed I was self-contained and autonomous. Even at sixteen. Even if I'm not going to be this person at twenty-five.

What's something a modern sixteen-year-old can do to resist that doesn't involve a tattoo? (Laughs.)

JASON: If we're being honest about who sixteen-year-olds are, we would see that they actually live in space of resistance. It's just that we adults tend to only see resistance as an *act* when I think these kids actually exist in a space of passive resistance. Sixteen-year-olds ain't thinking about the bullshit we were thinking about. I remember being sixteen and being homophobic, or that I didn't want to be seen with the goth kids. Sixteen-year-olds today, there's a different mentality. They can't understand how *we* can't get over the hatred. So many are like: here's my best friend, he lives on the other side of town, and he respects me and loves me and that's it. Teens don't understand how that's a problem. The internet, in all of its infinite bullshit, has also made the world smaller and less frightening. So seeing people who are different from them isn't that big of a deal. It's the adults. It's the insecurity of adults who create blockades for kids. What do I care that he lives in Mexico? What do I care that she's Muslim? So that is resistance. What they're actually resisting is the strong-arm tone of the government, but also the strong-arm tone of adultness. The fear of adulthood.

Kids always ask me about their version of rap music. The state of rap music. I tell them the same thing I always tell them: your rap music is your rap music. It belongs to you. If I liked it the way you do, you know you're not doing enough. You're not pushing hard enough. It's your *job* to piss me off with what you're making, and for me to say, "You're not good enough." So that's the point. So if I say I love all the music you're making, you should be disappointed.

Where do you look for hope these days?

JASON: The greatest part of this career is the moments I get to be with the kids, man. It's really difficult for me to be hopeless when I'm around thousands and thousands of young people ranging from third grade to college, and to listen to what they have to say, and watch them laugh and ask them

[38] MAUREEN JOHNSON

questions and figure out what's happening around them. There's no way I could be hopeless. They are the antidote. Even the fact that I write some pretty tough stuff—those books are full of kids who are whole. What we can learn is that, yes, there are kids who are dealing with things that should cause me to be hopeless. But the truth is, they are full human beings. So yes, the world is shit for them—but at the same time, you walk down 125th Street and you see kids dancing it out to no music. In a world that is music-less these kids are still finding rhythm.

I understand the temptation of hopelessness, but for me I feel a sense of responsibility and a sense of security we'll be okay. And not because of who's in office; because I know for a fact that there's a generational groundswell of young people who together are impenetrable—if all of us are doing our jobs by giving them the necessary legs, and not cutting them down, which we do all the time as adults.

You mentioned talking with and visiting thousands of teens a year. What is the top concern of teens today?

JASON: Easy. Donald Trump. The funny thing is: it's the top concern no matter where I've been. Even if *they're* not anti-Trump, it's still: what do you think, Jason? First question: "What do you think of Donald Trump and what he said about fill-in-the-blank?" When I travel to Germany, the first question is: is Donald Trump real? Italy. Germany. Everywhere I've been, it's: so is the Donald Trump thing a joke?

What do you wish teens were *more* concerned about?

JASON: The thing I want them to be thinking more about is—and the collective *we* should take the blame for this: I need teens to understand that

HOW I RESIST [39]

there's a double-edged sword with social media. I don't believe social media is bad, just that it can be dangerous. And I need young people to understand that. We've got to figure out how to rein it in, control it a little better. It's the Wild West.

So I say to them: listen, give yourself an hour. A break. An hour off of it. I have the same struggle. I force myself to go to the movies three times a week because it forces me to unplug.

If you can give yourself a half hour to unplug for just a second, I believe it will work in magnitudes. It's less about arguing with *what* they're posting, and more about us not addressing the addiction. Not just the addiction to scrolling, but the addiction to being praised.

When I was sixteen, my tattoo was going to be seen by the twenty people in my class. Nowadays, there are thousands of people who can see everything we do.

So as part of our resistance education, we occasionally need to resist our iPhones?

JASON: Absolutely. Resistance is about restraint, too.

Carolyn DeWitt is Rock the Vote's president and executive director, leading the organization's robust efforts to build political power for young people across the country. Before joining Rock the Vote as chief operating officer in 2015, Carolyn served as chief of staff for Pivot, a political communications firm, during the 2014 election cycle and coordinated surrogate media appearances for the 2012 Democratic National Convention in Charlotte. DeWitt has also spent time working with democracy-building efforts in South Africa and Kenya, and served as a senior international advisor to a youth political movement and potential presidential candidate in Madagascar.

FIVE THINGS TEENS CAN DO TO ENGAGE IN POLITICS BEFORE TURNING EIGHTEEN

Getting engaged in politics and building power for your community is about more than just voting. Even before you're old enough to register and cast a ballot yourself, there are plenty of opportunities to get engaged in politics, build political power, and take action on the issues important to you and your community. It's never too early to educate yourself about the voting process and learn who your elected officials are at the local, state, and national level, as well as the issues they can impact.

As young people, we can choose to sit on the sidelines or we can join together and fight for a future that works for us. Whether the most important issue to you is building a fair economy, fighting for racial justice and women's rights, combatting climate change, or preventing gun violence, you have a role to play in creating the change you want to see in the world.

Here are five ways YOU can get involved, even before your eighteenth birthday:

Get involved in a club or organization at your school or in your community: Whether you're running for a leadership position in student government, joining your school's Gay-Straight Alliance, or getting involved with the local 4-H club, there are plenty of opportunities to engage in your school or community and fight for what you believe in.

Pre-register to vote (if your state allows it): Pre-registering guarantees that you will automatically be able to cast a ballot as soon as you turn eighteen. Check to see if your state allows pre-registration at rockthevote .com, and take a couple minutes to fill out the form. If your state *doesn't* allow pre-registration yet, email your state legislator and urge them to empower teens to get registered early.

Figure out what issues you care about and learn who the key decision-makers are: Your history and social studies or civics classes in school are great places to start. Learn how local government functions and who decides the policies that impact your life or your community. For example, do you want to fight climate change? Go to usa.gov/local-governments and call or email your mayor or city council member. Let them know that you support stronger environmental policies and urge them to take action. If criminal justice reform is important to you, tell your local sheriff or district attorney to take action.

Help others get civically engaged: Even if you aren't old enough to vote yet, chances are that you have friends, neighbors, or family members who are. Using toolkits and resources or our volunteer sign-up form on rockthevote.com, you can help others get engaged by helping them register to vote and reminding them when there's an election. Offer to help educate them about the candidates on the ballot or the issues that are important to you. In some states, you can even volunteer as a poll worker on Election Day.

Volunteer for a campaign: Whether it's for a candidate who inspires you, a ballot initiative that you support, or even a new education bond to support your school, you don't have to be eighteen to volunteer for a campaign. Visit the campaign's website to sign up, and be a part of electing a new leader who will fight for the issues important to you—or getting your community to vote for a new law or policy.

HEBH JAMAL

Hebh Jamal is a visionary revolutionary leader. At the age of fifteen she became a well-known advocate in education reform known for her wisdom about the impact of injustice and her vision for the possibility of a transformed society. Hebh was featured in the New York Times article "Young Muslim Americans Are Feeling the Strain of Suspicion" for her perspective on the impact of Islamophobia on young Muslims and her vision for a more conscious, educated, and harmonious society. Since then, she has continued to be a voice for integrated, equitable schools in NYC and co-created the first-ever City-Wide Youth Council on School Integration run by IntegrateNYC4Me. She works toward fighting for the liberation of Palestinians and an end to Israeli occupation. She's a member of American Muslims for Palestine and her local SJP. Follow her on Twitter @hebh_jamal and Instagram @hebzter101.

As a seventeen-year-old, I am part of a generation that has lived through two wars and a financial crisis, and faces the burden of attending college as its costs skyrocket. Although I have no recollection of the stock market crash and am not immediately affected by the wars in Iraq and Afghanistan, those realities, and the political and economic system that created them, deeply affect my reality and future. I can't do anything about past events, but I can learn from history: my resistance is a product of past and current movements for equity and social justice. Like past and current activists, I face the challenges of trying to figure out how my resistance can be most effective.

As a Muslim-Palestinian-American, the hyphens that shape my identity have helped shape my efforts to resist injustice and envision a better world. As I have learned about Palestinian history and culture, and have visited relatives in Palestine and Jordan, I have become aware of the day-to-day impact of oppression on my family members and of the ongoing domination of Palestinian society and economy, enthusiastically supported by the American government. So when I think about resistance to injustice, I think about both domestic injustice—segregated schools, police shootings, destruction of the environment for profit, discrimination against marginalized people, attacks on immigrants, domination by the 1 percent—and

[48] MAUREEN JOHNSON

the injustice that the government supports elsewhere in my name. Thus, my resistance must encompass both.

The enormous scale of what we face in trying to create a just society for all people in the world can evoke confusion and frustration about being an activist. Where to start? Do I work within the system to change it? Do I work for another American revolution?

When I was younger, "revolution" first conjured up images of George Washington crossing the Delaware and later guerrillas hiding in the hills. More recently, I came to see it as a political uprising—seizing the existing power structures and directing them to the good of the people.

But the basis of more fundamental change may lie in thinking of revolution as a bottom-up grassroots process. Gaining control of local institutions, such as city council seats and state governments, can, in effect, revolutionize the larger system. In her book, *The Next American Revolution*, Grace Lee Boggs uses the analogy of physics to speak of activism and social change. Her Newtonian concept of the world makes individuals look for change not in grand terms but in smaller "organic connections" that become a means for the changes to bleed into greater levels of power. Boggs says that, in this way, "We are more likely to be sensitive to the dynamics of the system, and thus more effective."

This is not incrementalism. Our collective effort in fighting for affordable neighborhoods, for higher education, and for a peaceful, sustainable world, allows us not to depend on one spectacular event to create long-lasting change. Our involvement creates the awareness that Boggs eloquently refers to. Working locally can create consensus based on the wants and needs of our communities. At the same time, thinking globally means confronting our representatives around issues such as climate change, ongoing wars, and ending support for Israel's oppression of Palestinians, as well as, for example, making collective decisions to use our purchasing power to boycott companies (and countries) as needed.

For grassroots action to be revolutionary and not merely incremental, we must keep thinking about our long-term goals of fighting destructive power structures and how our actions help us to reach these goals. When organizing, it is easy for time to be consumed as there is always work to be done. Activism can leave little time to simply think. The idea of deliberately taking time to think seems simple, yet it is the most challenging thing for me to do on a continuous basis. Tony Judt, at the last moments of his life, wrote about the importance of a "moral narrative." I try to think about the overall moral narrative that my actions contribute to. It is important to humanize all struggles by remembering who is affected and how they are impacted. Taking time to think deeply about one's advocacy makes a more productive advocate. How I resist is therefore deeply affected by how much I am willing to think.

While building a grassroots effort, we can't become submissive to a capitalist mentality that encourages focusing on individual "leaders." If one starts an organization or has a "following," it is important not to succumb to constant use of the word "I." Although I understand the importance of individual narratives, movements are more powerful when understood as collaborative efforts. Dealing with media attention has been a constant struggle for me. On one hand, I understand there are not many Muslim women getting attention for their activism. On the other hand, I fear that too much focus on my story steers the focus away from the issues I'm trying to bring to light. Instead, what I find most productive is sharing important moments with colleagues or asking them for help.

I am forced to think on a daily basis about how and why I resist. As Grace Lee and James Boggs wrote years ago, an American revolution will be distinctively American, not a copy of past revolutions. Through our daily activism, we are in the process of shaping what that revolution will look like. Like all revolutions, it will expand the meaning of being human (and, indeed, the meaning of being part of an ecosystem that includes all forms of life and the earth itself). My struggles to figure out how to be effective are one small part of this. But what I know is that we cannot view resistance and creating a new world as a side gig. Our lives and the fate of the world itself may depend on our success.

JAVIER MUÑOZ

Javier Muñoz is an American actor and singer. Muñoz is best known for his performances on Broadway as Usnavi in the 2008 musical *In the Heights* and as Alexander Hamilton in the 2015 musical *Hamilton* where he shared the title role with the show's creator, Lin-Manuel Miranda. Javier Muñoz has had the great honor to perform *Hamilton* for both President Obama and First Lady Michelle Obama. He is the recipient of the 2007 Drama Desk Award, the 2016 OUT100 Breakout of the Year Award, the 2016 GMHC Howard Ashman Award, the 2016 HOLA Dare To Go Beyond Award, and the 2017 Lambda Legal National Liberty Award. Follow him on Twitter @JMunozActor.

What was your activism life like before you took on the role of Alexander Hamilton?

JAVIER: It was a lot of literacy work and work with HIV causes. I hate to say it like this, but it was simpler, gentler, kinder . . . it was work that didn't feel so life or death. Or it felt life or death in a different way—we're talking about raising money for HIV/AIDS organizations. That's obviously life or death. But there was light, there was levity to those times. And now times feel so desperate, so pressured. The climate of the day-to-day feels like everything matters, everything's important. So there's a different purpose going into activism now. It's a different voice, it's a different energy.

You literally go onstage and enact a revolution every night over, what, three hours?

JAVIER: Three hours, yes.

That's a lot of energy to be generating every night.

JAVIER: It is!

[54] MAUREEN JOHNSON

Why do you think *Hamilton* resonates with so many?

JAVIER: Well, I think the first thing is the medium in which Lin has written it, in the form of rap. The music of the show is tantalizing, it's exciting, it's riveting. You just want to hear it. You just want to experience it. And then you've got this character. Hamilton, as he's depicted here, is this classic rebel that everybody loves. He works his way from the ground up, and fights his way through, and he wins! Everybody wants to see that story. Everybody wants to cheer that guy on.

We all have an innate desire to make a difference, to make an impact, to be seen, to be heard, to leave behind something better than what we're brought into. I think we all actually have that. Whether we do anything with it or not is a different story. I think innately every human being wants to do good. I really do believe that. What that good *looks* like is a different story. I think Hamilton taps into the hero in everybody. I mean he's a scrappy guy.

Do you love him?

JAVIER: I do love him! I love playing this character!

He's a scamp.

JAVIER: He is. While he is that, he's also . . . I mean, the things he accomplished are immense. They are tremendous. I do admire that about him.

The diversity of this cast, I think, has also changed America.

JAVIER: I hope it did, I really do. Let's just talk about theater as a genre for a second. I think it's really difficult now to cast anything in the face of

Hamilton and not make it diverse, to not cast the best actor for the role as opposed to keeping it limited to a certain ethnicity. Or even gender. And I think it's catapulted casting in a different direction.

But has it changed America? I don't know. I would like to think that the diversity of the cast of *Hamilton* certainly inspires minorities across the country to find deeper self-worth, to find self-empowerment, to see themselves represented in a positive way and know that that's as valid a message as any other negative message they've ever gotten their entire lives. That it's a *more* powerful and valid message. I'd like to think that's happening. I'm in this bubble of *Hamilton* so I don't know yet. I haven't traveled outside of it for two and a half years. I think that's something I may learn when I'm done.

What I'm grateful for are the conversations that are happening, because at least we're talking about diversity. At least we're bringing it up and shining a light on it. You can't escape it. You're sitting and watching it for three hours. In your face! Diversity!

[Editor's note: On November 18, 2016, then newly elected Vice President Pence attended a performance of Hamilton. *The cast, after finding out that Vice President Pence was in the audience, had to decide how to handle the situation. In the end, they opted to give a speech, which was delivered during the curtain call by actor Brandon Victor Dixon, who played Aaron Burr.]*

You were playing Hamilton throughout the election season of 2016.

JAVIER: Yes.

[56] MAUREEN JOHNSON

The performance where Mike Pence was in the audience . . . can you tell me about what happened that night?

JAVIER: Yes, sure. (*Deep breath.*) I break things down in terms of before Pence and after Pence, because it became an entirely different thing after he came to the show. That night, I got here around 7. 7:15 is usually my wig call. At 7:15 there was going to be a meeting in the basement with our lead producer and that meeting was intended to announce to the cast that Pence was coming. I couldn't be there because I was getting ready for the show. So stage management came into my dressing room to tell me the news. And I think the fear on the part of management, both company management and stage management, was that we would walk out. Which was an impulse; I won't lie, that was certainly an impulse. But the greater impulse was an opportunity to be great. This was an opportunity to literally demonstrate not only the greatness of the story but the greatness of the diversity of this cast, how great we are at *what we do,* and that in and of itself became a statement.

I'll preface this by saying I'm still to this day impressed and grateful that he stayed. He stayed. He heard it. He watched. He heard our message. And to his credit, right? Because if you're staying you're watching me for three hours and I'm literally the antithesis of everything he believes in politically. That's a choice to stay there and experience the story. So I still feel gratitude that he came to the table that way.

But the energy in the building was overwhelming. People were very emotional about it, about his being here. Really, I saw it as an opportunity to be great. That was the energy I kept putting out . . . "We're on fire tonight, let's give the best show that we absolutely can." It was a hard show to do. It was hard on the heart, it was hard on the mind. I had to compartmentalize everything in order to execute the show and not keep thinking about him being out there in the house.

When we came to the curtain call, we were supposed to do our regular bow, present the musical director, do another bow, and then give the speech. We did our first bow, presented the musical director, and I could hear Brandon say, "He's leaving. We should just do it now, let's just do it now." So we went right into the speech, and he stayed. He stayed and listened to the message.

The fallout from that is a whole other story. It catapulted the show, and particularly me and Brandon, into a spotlight that was very aggressive toward us, and that's a mild way of putting things. We had to increase security here in the building. We got hate mail, death threats over social media, death threats sent to the theater, phone calls came in, etc. Our security had to be doubled. Brandon and I couldn't really go anywhere without security being around. We had to be walked to the cars or to the train station, or have security meet us at the train station to walk us into the building. And the hate was real. Endless, endless letters I've received telling me why I should die, how I should die, telling me that God hates me and all the reasons why, and all the reasons I should be punished, and how I should be punished. Very specific stuff. I'm talking about eight-page letters.

And that's how things were. It was a very turbulent time. But I think any celebrity or public person is given a platform whether they want it or not. You're given a light and a microphone and the things that you care about get amplified by the nature of what you're doing. That existed already with *Hamilton* and then add this political climate, add Pence coming to the show. I saw it as an opportunity to really dig into what I believe in, what I stand for, and not be cowed or shamed or embarrassed or intimidated into

[58] MAUREEN JOHNSON

being silent. Given all the violent language that was coming at me and at the show, you've got two choices: you can either hide or you can literally face it. I just felt that it was an opportunity to face it. And my activism, which was already present, tripled. Now it's about ebbing and flowing, picking and choosing when and what to do so that I can support and help amplify our message as long as he's in office.

Currently, we're really getting into a conversation about what America is, about the founding fathers, about our past. We're asking things like, *What is America*? What does the Constitution say? Who wrote it?

JAVIER: One of the things that stands out to me when you bring that up are the Schuyler sisters talking about "women in the sequel." That line alone . . . we've gone centuries and have we really discussed that? That it's *men men men men men* all over our founding documents? Are we finally discussing that? Are we really? Is this helping propel that conversation? Amongst all the other things, I sort of dig anytime I see a new History channel TV show or whatever history program that focuses on our founding fathers and they focus on them being slave owners, and they talk about that as opposed to sweeping it under the rug. Let's *talk* about the fact that they were slave owners.

And that they had the slavery conversation *at the time,* and they walked away from it.

JAVIER: Right. I think the impact of this show on things like that is tremendous. Tremendous. People always mention that the timing of this show was perfect. And I say, "Actually, no. Anytime that the show was created would have been the right time." These are age-old issues that we had in our country that we are finally looking at square in the eye. This show would have helped propel that conversation at any point. So I don't think it's perfect timing. I think the show itself is that good. What Lin created is that potent and that real, and raw, and honest.

One of the lines from the show that I always think about is "Let's steal their cannons." Let's do that. Let's steal their cannons.

JAVIER: That's everything that happened in Charlottesville, right? That's real confrontation, that's real engagement. I don't think it was empowering to anyone in that situation who was a white supremacist or was from the KKK or promoting Nazi ideology. That moment in our history pulled the rug out from underneath them. Really, I think that. In the way it brought the rest of us together, that's tremendous.

Momentum toward compassion, understanding, supporting one another . . . realizing that a person's struggle, though it's not mine, is important and I need to defend them and they're going to defend me . . . this is how we go forward. Cannons being metaphorical, I feel like it really pulled their power away from them and their hate. The way we all really rallied around that was huge. That's stealing their cannons.

A lot of kids now, they're going to grow up and this political climate is going to be their baseline. This is what they're going to see as normal. Do you have any message for those kids?

JAVIER: I hope there's enough energy and momentum in opposition to the rhetoric and the principles and the very blatant hate that this administration embodies. I hope there's enough opposition, enough strong voices to help young people see that that's not the right way to be. The way we stand strong in our diversity, supporting one another, standing up for the little guy, uniting against the things that are just blatantly unfair, protecting each

[60] MAUREEN JOHNSON

other, having compassion for each other . . . I hope that *those* things are so prevalent, that that's what sticks with them.

And I hope that if anyone like Trump comes up again they'll recognize it. Don't forget this guy. Don't forget what he said. Don't forget what it looks like when someone like this comes around. That's my hope: that once he's gone we won't sweep it under the rug. We've got to keep looking at it. Because this will happen again if we try to forget about it.

Jennifer Weiner is the #1 New York Times bestselling author of fifteen books, including the novels Good in Bed, In Her Shoes, *and* Who Do You Love, *the middle-grade trilogy* The Littlest Bigfoot, *and the essay collection* Hungry Heart, *which was nominated for the 2017 PEN/Diamonstein-Spielvogel Award. She is a contributing opinion writer for* The New York Times. *She lives in Philadelphia with her family. Follow her on Twitter @JenniferWeiner.*

THE LUCKY ONES

When my daughter's second-grade class tackled persuasive writing, Phoebe did not need any help finding a subject. "Dear Donald Trump," Phoebe wrote. "I am writing for you to Come to your Senses and see what are you Doing to this country." She questioned his confidence that a wall would keep Mexicans out ("Haven't you heard of planes?") and argued against his hate for "Hispanics and Muslims." "You may have convinced yourself but you have Not Convinced Me," was how Phoebe ended her missive, which I proudly emailed to family and friends.

On Election Day, I marched both of my daughters, the enthusiastic younger and the just-let-me-do-my-homework elder, to the polls. In our diverse Philadelphia neighborhood, the mood in the church where we vote was ebullient. People were passing around boxes of pizza and chocolates, smiling as they thanked us for voting. Together, the three of us depressed the button after I'd selected Hillary Clinton for president. We walked home wrapped in a comfortable blanket of conviction, certain that she had it in the bag.

The next morning, Phoebe bounded out of bed. "Did she win?" she asked, and she must have seen the answer on our faces because she started to cry. Her two best buddies are both adopted—one girl, born in New Jersey, has two dads, the other came from Ethiopia. "Will Miriam's dads still be allowed to be her parents?" Phoebe cried. "Will Degitu's parents have to send her back?"

I consoled her as best I could. I didn't lie. Her friends would be fine, I told her. People like us, and her friends' parents, people with good educations, and connections, and money, were not the ones likely to be hurt by Trump's policies. We are lucky, I told my daughter, who looked at me through brimming eyes and demanded, "Well, what about the people who aren't?"

Like many Americans, I hadn't thought much about the cozy and politically affirming world I'd created for myself, the bubble in which I lived, until I realized that there were sixty-three million Americans who'd happily pulled the lever or pushed the button for a privileged, multiply-bankrupt and twice-divorced reality television star who'd been caught on tape musing about grabbing women by the pussy. In my confusion and my pain, I set out to understand these people, reading approximately eight hundred think pieces and hot takes, each of which had a different explanation for Trump's victory. It's the economy, one argued. No, it's the misogyny, said another. One piece pointed at racism, another at identity politics, another at voter disenfranchisement, or James Comey, or her emails, or the media.

The arguments I found the most convincing were the ones by Arlie Russell Hochschild and Jill Filipovic.

Hochschild, a sociologist, spent five years embedded in Trumplandia, and emerged with the concept of line-jumpers. White middle-class and working-class voters look at themselves as hard workers who "play by the rules," while the government sides with women and minorities and immigrants, beneficiaries of a plethora of programs and subsidies and special assists. These white voters look out at the world and see people unlike them getting ahead while people like them have to work harder and harder just to stay in place.

Then there was the lady situation. "For all of American history, white men have been both the dominant group and the default one," Filipovic wrote in *The New York Times*. "It was mostly white men in charge, and it was white male experiences and norms against which all others found themselves contrasted and defined."

And now? Women have found many paths to success. "No one bats an eye if we cut our hair short, wear pants, pay with a credit card in our own name, win on the soccer field, or buy our own home," Filipovic wrote. Meanwhile, "Men haven't gained nearly as much flexibility. The world has changed around them, but many have stayed stuck in the past."

I think of what Barack Obama said after the Obergefell ruling, which made marriage equality the law of the land. It was a day of exultant celebration for my family, especially my mom, Fran, and her partner, Clair. "Progress on this journey often comes in small increments," Obama said. "Sometimes two steps forward, one step back, compelled by the persistent effort of dedicated citizens. And then sometimes there are days like this, when that slow, steady effort is rewarded with justice that arrives like a thunderbolt."

To my people—my daughters, my mother, my neighbors, my daughters' teachers and classmates—all this progress has been fantastic; the thunderbolt was welcome. To the Tea Party voters and the mired white men, it must have felt like some cruel god had pressed the fast-forward button and landed them in a horror-movie version of the future. Suddenly, gays can marry. Suddenly, you can't joke around about the body parts of your female colleagues. Suddenly, it's worse to be the junior-high kid who makes fun of gay classmates than it is to be gay. What about me, asks the angry white man, whose full-time job's been reduced to part-time because his employer can't afford rising insurance premiums and whose Walmart greeters started to say "Happy Holidays" and not "Merry Christmas"? What about us, asks his wife, who'd rather be part-time but has to work full-time because her family needs her benefits, who's seen a brother or a son sink into addiction because

[66] MAUREEN JOHNSON

there are too few jobs and not enough hope? Donald Trump figured out how to talk to those voters, through speech and through winks and dog-whistles, through what he said and what he re-tweeted and what he didn't say or didn't condemn. Trump's Make America Great Again slogan told those mired white guys and their daughters and wives that it wasn't their fault that they'd slipped, that a great America was one with them on top, and that Trump was the man to put them there.

The first president I can remember is Ronald Reagan, which means that the first president Phoebe will remember is Donald Trump, which makes me sadder than I can say. That was the thought that kept me going as I hauled my middle-aged self from Philadelphia to Washington and walked the same route I'd marched as a college student protesting for abortion rights in 1990, past women thirty years my senior holding signs that said I CAN'T BELIEVE I'M STILL MARCHING FOR THIS SHIT. That is the thought that animates me when I sort through the stories I'm going to tell them when they come up against classmates or coworkers who see things Donald Trump's way and want to live in his America.

I'll tell my daughters what it was like when I was earning sixteen thousand dollars at my first job and my crap insurance did not cover birth control, and how Planned Parenthood was there to give me checkups and the Pill. I'll tell them about what it was like to point out inequities and gender imbalance in the world of publishing and to hear not rational arguments or fact-based rebuttals but, instead, that I was strident, or ugly, or self-centered, or annoying, or that I just wanted attention for my own unworthy work.

I'll tell my daughters that when my mother was a young woman, the only way to have a family was to marry a man, and that it was illegal for gay men and women to love who they wanted to love. I'll tell them how, just a few generations ago, my grandparents and great-grandparents were immigrants, who came here from Poland and Russia, fleeing poverty and op-

HOW I RESIST [67]

pression and anti-Semitism, hoping to make a better life for themselves and their children.

I'll tell them that we've got a choice between an America that's generous and one that's stingy; an America that embraces its best impulses or one that yields to its worst; an America that rises to the occasion or an America that sinks to the lowest common denominator. I'll teach them not to shy away from debate or dissent, and will arm them with the sense of what is just and what is right that my own mother passed down to me. It will be their job—just as it's mine right now—to leave the world a better place than when they found it, to push for change and for progress, to speak truth to power, to know how good they've got it. My girls are the lucky ones. Their job—our job—is to stand up for everyone who isn't as lucky, to know, as Jews recite every Passover, that while one of us is still in bondage, none of us are free.

John Paul Brammer is a queer Mexican-American writer and speaker who hails from rural Oklahoma and is currently based in New York City. His work has been published in The Guardian, Slate, BuzzFeed, NBC, and many other outlets. He is also an advice columnist despite his status as a general human disaster. He can be found on Twitter and on Instagram @jpbrammer.

LETTER TO A SENSITIVE BROWN QUEER

You're standing there, nine years old, in the middle of the fabric store in Wichita Falls, Tejas—a Hispanic boy holding leopard print in one hand and hideous fur trim in the other. Sorry, mijo, but it's hideous. I promise you develop a more discerning eye for aesthetics later. But that doesn't matter right now. What matters right now is that you're a boy picking out fabrics, and this is a problem for the fabric store lady. She's got a smile on her face, but she's crushing your soul in the palm of her hand.

"Isn't this a girl thing?" she says, pointing an acrylic nail to the spotted yard of jotería in your hand. It's a punch to your chubby gut. Not that you know what a punch to the gut really feels like, of course. You've never been in a fight in your whole life, not even a tussle. You wouldn't hurt a fly. You cry when you stub your toe. These are facts.

Your sister and your cousins are running around the store, freedom in their hair as they skip down the aisles, picking out patterns for their fabric lampshades. That's why your auntie brought you all here—to make your own lamps. She saw it in a magazine and thought it would be fun. You asked, in an uncharacteristic act of bravery, if you could make one too. With the girls. To which your auntie responded, "Sure."

Watching the girls in the store, you are acutely reminded of how old ladies are always stopping them on the street. "They must be sisters!" they

[72] MAUREEN JOHNSON

coo, while you stand awkwardly to the side in your Pokémon shirt from the Husky Kids section of Walmart. "Look at their eyes!"

Yes, everyone got the hazel eyes except you and your mama. You got brown, like most people. Prettiness feels like something you've been locked out of—while the girls browse the jewelry rack at Claire's, you sit outside on the bench. While they braid their hair, you get the Caesar cut, also at Walmart, because where else? When Great-Aunt Gloria visits like a Mexican ghost that appears approximately once a year, the girls get "qué linda" while you get "panzón." Fatso. You don't even know that panzón means fatso until, like, years later. That's how slow the burn is.

Your life is full of characters like the fabric store lady, dungeon bosses standing between you and fabulosity. And you always seem to lose. One little remark, and all the hearts in your health bar disappear. *Critical hit.* Boom. You're dead.

And so you do what you always do when met with resistance. You cry. Right there in the middle of the fabric store, faux fur and hideous trim in your hands, making a scene in front of God and Selena Quintanilla in Heaven and all the customers. You cry.

You're no stranger to crying. You cry like it's going out of style. You cried when you got picked last for soccer at recess, even though you hate soccer and you're aware that you suck at it. You cried when, after a productive session of sketching dresses and gowns you were particularly proud of, you asked your mama if you could be a designer, and she said, "Of course, baby. But I wouldn't tell anyone." You cried when you told your uncle you wanted to see *The Fast and the Furious* instead of *The Princess Diaries,* even though you really wanted to see *The Princess Diaries.* Your uncle didn't even do shit, man. He just asked a question and out came the waterworks.

And here you are, crying again, because the fabric store lady decided to interrogate you like it's part of her job description (it's not). You're getting the judgmental looks now, some serious mal de ojo. *What a weird, misbehaved boy,* they must be thinking. *What a crybaby.* That's what people are always thinking.

How could they know that you're not really crying over the lamp? Well, okay, it's a little bit about the lamp. You really want a lamp. True. But there's a lot more to it than that. There's a big picture in your head. You painted it with your mind's brush. It's incomplete, but you see it in brilliant flashes of clarity. Not in the moments when you're sneaking your mama's *Vogue* up the stairs to your room, or in the moments after, when she asks you if you've seen it and you sheepishly put it back in the magazine rack in the bathroom. But in the moments when you're good and lost in it. You see a world that has room for you, where you can create, and live, and be.

And every time something like this happens, when someone stops you just as you're about to step into that colorful nirvana and says, "No, not you," it feels like you've been damned to a bland, ill-fitting *always.* You'll *always* be on the outside looking in. You'll *always* be in your baggy clothes, watching other people be beautiful. You'll *always* be in your room, sketchbooks stashed under your bed, wishing you were someone else. Because you're a boy. And boys can't be pretty, and boys can't pick out fabrics, and boys certainly can't cry.

Your auntie comes over. She would have stooped down, but she's mad short, so she just sort of looks at you at eye level. The sentiment is there, though. She asks, "Mijo, do you still want to make a lamp?"

And here's where I've got some advice for you, because here is where you have a choice. The road forks ahead of you, and things can go one of two ways.

One. You can drop the fabrics right there. You can wipe away your tears and suck it up, like people are always telling you to do. You can suck up your gut, too. You can suck it all up, and you can hold it in for the rest of your life like they want you to, and it will hurt like hell and make you tired, but people won't look at you weird anymore. That's it. That's all you get out of it.

Two. You can nod your head yes, puffy-eyed and sniffling. You'll be embarrassed, and a little uncomfortable. But at the end, you'll have something to show for it. Something you made, because you wanted to make it. You can accept that crying is just something you do. That it's how you heal. That maybe crying is magic, even—a process that draws from the inner ocean of your spirit and washes the hurt away. You can resist the people who'd try to drain it and replace it with nada, because they're holding it all in, and they're mad that you're not.

My advice is that you always choose **two.** Even if it's hard sometimes. Even if people look at you weird. Even if it makes you embarrassed sometimes, and even if people tell you you're going the wrong way. Because in time, I promise if you keep walking, you'll get there. To that place you've always wanted to be, where you can make of yourself anything you want, where you can skip down the aisles and fill your basket with materials, and it will feel like freedom.

But for now, as you ride home with your cousins, snot still running from your nose, take the time to smile, mijo. Tell your sister how pretty her lamp is. Thank her when she says, "Yours too." When you get back to the house, set it on your nightstand as the sun goes down. When it's good and dark, turn the light on. Take in the yellow warmth of its glow, and be happy with what you've made.

Daniel J. Watts has appeared in eight Broadway shows, including Hamilton, In the Heights, After Midnight, and Memphis, in addition to various roles in TV/film including Blindspot (NBC), Vinyl (HBO), and Tracy Morgan's comedy series The Last O.G. His concert "The Jam" is a spoken word/storytelling experience fusing a live band, song, dance, and multimedia where he encourages audiences to focus on social similarities opposed to differences. As an educator, Watts has also served as an adjunct professor of NYU's Tisch New Studio. He earned his BFA from the Elon University Music Theatre Program, and is the recipient of the 2011 Young Alumnus Award. Find him at www.wattswords.com or @dwattswords.

THE CLAP BACK

That clap back be on beat
2 & 4 to be exact

Since slavery was abolished in 1865
We have long since been no longer responsible for your comfort
We were divided and in bondage
Now we're uniting and bonding
No longer too afraid to follow our family trees for fear of finding bodies
swinging from their branches
No more sorrys
We be blatantly unapologetic now
Tubman underground & Parks on the bus unapologetic
Davis, Baldwin, & Scott-Heron unapologetic
Assata Shakur on a beach in Cuba unapologetic
Tyson with the black trunks
Williams sisters with the beads
Ali anti-war
Tommie and John at the '68 Olympics
Beyoncé, Solange, and JAY-Z's elevator music
Kendrick at the Grammys
Kaepernick on the field

[78] MAUREEN JOHNSON

Simone playing all the black keys
Auntie Maxine reclaiming her time
Obama's State of the Union 6 unapologetic
No matter what Stacey Dash or Sheriff David Clarke might think
This black is no more new
Than watermelon is indigenous to Alabama
Harvested by King Tut himself
Watermelon was born in Africa
Just like everything else
Yeah that clap back be on beat
2 & 4 to be exact
And oooooo ya'll done messed up now
you
took our drums back then
but gave us Twitter today

shouts to @deray
@shaunKing
and @MHarrisPerry
Now we're memeing Fortune 500 companies, award shows,
and celebrities into apologies they
never intended to give
#PaulaDeen #CheddarBayBiscuits #OscarsSoWhite
#AudraMcDonaldvsBillOReilly
These ain't reparations but we'll take 'em for now
I tell you
That clap back be on beat
2 & 4 to be exact
now we killing it

rhyming in triplets
Love or hate it yeah your children are feeling it
We got your kids
Bih
We got your kids
We got your kids
listening to Drake and dabbin' on 'em in the background at major
sporting events
We got your kids pissed off at the police too
We got your kids dying to be a part of a culture that has always been
inclusive as long as you're down for
the cause
We got your kids down for the cause
We got your kids willing to give up their privilege to level the playing field
We got your kids reminding you that we are your kids too
Your neglected children with different mamas, but the same daddy
Different hues and textures of hair, but yeah we got the same daddy
Different socioeconomic statuses, but mmmmm the same daddy
And the same dirty-ass Uncle Sam that was giving out cash, land, and
pursuits of happiness to our fairer
skinned siblings while fondling us inappropriately behind closed doors
The doors are open now
The light has been shed
The question is, Will you hold him accountable like Cosby?
Uncle Sam roofied all of Flint, Michigan and you actually saw that water

Oooo that clap back be on beat
2 & 4 to be exact
This is that clap back

[80] MAUREEN JOHNSON

That "get you in check quick"
"get you right together"
that "gathered that ass"
That "think before you speak" because we got four hundred years of
the dozens we've been waiting to
unleash
Way beyond slave ships, chains, whips, lynchings, water fountains, lunch
counters, school boards,
misogyny, housing codes, bank loans, taxicabs, country clubs, crack, stop
and frisk, mass incarceration,
and bang bang shoot 'em up policing
But "Yo mama so white her husband wants to make sure that you don't
fall in love with me." (Repeat.)
And who can blame them? Who among us would wish terrorism
upon their
descendants? What twisted patriarch wants to pass down a cursed
heirloom—an antique dominant gene
that has been historically and systematically stolen and locked up for
"safekeeping"?
Who wants to be black other than black people?
Who wants it beyond the culture? Who wants it beyond the crossovers
and the touchdown celebrations,
and the cornrows, and the fresh/dope/swag/slay? Who wants it beyond
the vocal runs, and the neck
rolls and the "Bye Felicia," and the soul food and the trap beat and
rhythm? Somebody tell me who wants to
appropriate this skin—this skin with far more legacies than bronzer,
tanning booths, and sun-kissed
vacations in the Caribbean?
This is going to hurt me more than it hurts you.

HOW I RESIST [81]

"I only whoop ya cuz I love ya."
But do you love me?
Do you love me?
Do you love me?
Do you love me?
Show me

ALI STROKER

Ali Stroker, the Glee *and* Glee Project *star, made history as the first actress in a wheelchair to appear on a Broadway stage, in Deaf West's revival of* Spring Awakening. *Ali has performed at the Kennedy Center and in New York at Town Hall and Lincoln Center. Stroker has a recurring character on the ABC drama* Ten Days in the Valley. *She is a cochair of Women Who Care, which supports United Cerebral Palsy of NYC, and Be More Heroic, an anti-bullying campaign, in addition to her work with ARTS InsideOut, which empowers women and children affected by AIDS in South Africa. Follow her on Instagram and Twitter @alistroker.*

When in your life were you first called to resist?

ALI: See, that word doesn't resonate for me. (*Laughs.*) Growing up with a disability, my experience was I didn't want to rock the boat more than I already was. I felt like I was already creating some discomfort for the world. As I got older and more mature, and my mind grew, I realized that that was not the case. That I was not creating discomfort.

I had to sort of shift it so that I could build my confidence, and I did that by learning. Through theater I found that I was accepted. And that being different was to my advantage. But that took a long time. I grew up in a really beautiful upper middle class white community, and I identify with being upper middle class and white and beautiful (laughs), and also not normal.

One of your signature phrases, as a nationally recognized advocate for so many causes, is "Make your limitations your opportunities." But limitations are still hard. How do you not turn bitter?

ALI: It's about having the right people around you. I call that having the right "home team."

[86] MAUREEN JOHNSON

My dad is a coach. My family was my home team; my brother also has a disability, so I didn't feel alone in having challenges.

But when I came to NYU, my world definitely shifted, and I realized that I could not assume that anyone understood or that they were going to accept me. That was a big, "Oh." So that's when I learned how to advocate and how to articulate. Because I don't always think it's advocating. Sometimes I think it's about articulating.

That's interesting. Can you tell me a little more about advocating vs. articulating?

ALI: Advocating for me has been learning how to get my needs met. Articulating means . . . I hate the word "explaining," because that is something I have resisted, in my life. Because the world always wants an explanation. Why are you in a wheelchair? Why are you injured? Why are you that way?

I think I can say this on behalf of the disabled community: there seems to be a desire from the world for us to explain ourselves. So "articulating" means to describe in a way that the able-bodied world can understand the experience. And that has been a part of my work. I do a lot of speaking gigs, and I've been playing more with the idea of being an activist, because I don't identify as that.

You are feeling more and more like an activist, but you don't identify with the word "resistance"?

ALI: I don't want to march in a parade and picket and write letters. That's not where I feel where I'm strongest. I feel like I'm strongest in speaking out. What I'm learning about advocating is that people are willing to listen, but they're not always willing to act. I have things happen to me every day. I just ordered food to go at a place that's inaccessible. It's a constant decision about whether I want to be an advocate or an activist, even if I go out for a drink. This is why it's so complicated—I do want to just be normal.

(Laughing.) It's a complicated and layered experience when you're looked to as an activist and a leader, and actually taking that on.

What would you tell your younger self in her darker moments of feeling the world was up against her?

ALI: I'm hesitant about some of this, because my college has ultimately been so supportive of me, but when I first arrived at NYU, I had some resistance to me. Which was really upsetting at the time, but I look back on it as one of the greatest introductions to my adult life. They told me I couldn't take the dance curriculum, but I was there for musical theater. My advice: in all of the success, there is going to be an equal amount of rejection. And that is a part of being who you are; being an artist; and being someone who wants to create change and be at the forefront of it.

I took the dance class. And it took weeks and months of patience with people who were scared. They were afraid of what it might mean to have somebody like me in their class. They were looking at it as: this is an able-bodied experience, and I looked as it as: this is the most important experience, because I need to know my body more than anyone else.

Your optimism really jumps out at me. Can you tell me about that point of view?

ALI: I got hurt when I was two. I was part of a car accident, and my brother got injured, and my mom was driving. And what I experienced was that

[88] MAUREEN JOHNSON

everyone who surrounded my family in that time of trauma was telling us we can do it. So it's deep inside of me: in any challenging situation, a positive can always be found. A light can always be found.

When my boyfriend picks up *The New York Times* every morning outside of our apartment, and we look at the headlines together, it is beyond disturbing. However, every day I have to go out into the world and make a choice. Do I want to be disturbed—sometimes, yes, because it's motivating at times for change. But oftentimes, in order for me to make positive change in the world, I need to feel good. I can't do it from anger and frustration.

I know what it's like to feel really, really shitty. So that choice of happiness is pretty intentional. I think it's a choice. For me, the positive has always been where I feel most powerful.

Who would play you in the musical of your life?

ALI: A young actress in a wheelchair.

So, you?

ALI: Me, but I hope there are many, many more actresses in wheelchairs that are coming up that want to pursue this wild and crazy business and believe that it is possible for them. And that the producers of the musical of my life would not even considering putting some able-bodied person who just looks like me in a wheelchair for that role.

Shaina Taub is a songwriter and performer, currently an artist-in-residence at the Public Theater's Joe's Pub. She is a winner of the Fred Ebb Award, the Jonathan Larson Grant, and the Billie Burke Ziegfeld Award. She has performed with the New York Pops at Carnegie Hall and was featured in Lincoln Center's American Songbook series. Her musical adaptations of Twelfth Night and As You Like It were commissioned and produced by the Public Theater as part of their Public Works initiative. She starred in both productions, as Feste and Jaques, respectively. Audra McDonald and Sutton Foster have performed her music, and she wrote the theme song for Julie Andrews's Netflix series, Julie's Greenroom, sung on the show by Sara Bareilles. She's writing a new musical about the American women's suffrage movement. www.shainataub.com.

WHEN

Music, Lyrics, and
Vocal Arrangement by
SHAINA TAUB

KC Green created the "This is fine" dog meme. The one everyone uses to ignore the problem. The one that keeps being brought up again and again. He's very sorry.

part of the problem

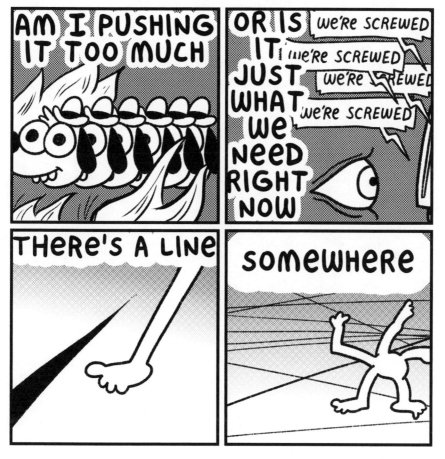

kc green

Dan Sinker is the cohost of Says Who *podcast, the author of the @MayorEmanuel Twitter account, and was the founding editor of the underground culture magazine* Punk Planet. *For a day job he helps journalists be awesome.*

MAKING STUFF THAT MATTERS

Sometimes a hashtag isn't enough. Sometimes you need to take action in the real world and you need something physical and real to make your statements. Maybe it's putting together a little zine about birth control options because your school stopped teaching them. Maybe it's taking some woodcuts you've made and converting them into a projection you'll use to shine BLACK LIVES MATTER across that busy bridge in town. Maybe it's building a huge Trump puppet sitting on a toilet with the words HOME POOPER eight feet high—please??—that you'll bring to a weekend march. Making stuff like this—things that can get noticed and get your message across—is amazing and YOU—yes, you—can make it happen.

Sure, you may not be an expert but that should never stop you from just going for it. As someone who started making things at your age and went on to build all kinds of things I had no idea how to do when I started, I'm going to step you through some of the doubts I struggle with or hear from others and get you moving toward making.

How can I make something if I don't know how to do it?

If you can't do something until you're good at it, how will you ever start? You won't! You've been told so many times that you need to be an expert to do something. But you know what? You don't! Sometimes you just need to

[112] MAUREEN JOHNSON

jump in, think of the thing you want to make, and start figuring out how to do it. Find something similar and take it apart—this is super useful if you're trying to print a little booklet or zine when the page counts are going to be all wacky when you fold and staple them. Check out YouTube videos: "How to make . . ." and then every keyword imaginable around your idea. A big Trump HOME POOPER puppet might not be findable but "how to make a giant puppet" will deliver a starting point. Find that tech-minded kid at the media lab at your school and ask her some questions. The most important tool you can have when you're making anything is curiosity. Start figuring it out and get going!

What if it's too hard to make fancy?

We live in a world that is super high-polish and that can be really intimidating when you're starting to make stuff. Nothing you make is going to be as perfect as your iPhone or as shiny as a new pair of shoes. That's OK! Something that is rough and works to get your point across is amazing! Honestly, it's better that way. Look: making things perfect is super hard. But "perfect" is such an impossible standard you shouldn't be holding yourself to. Make stuff scrappy, make stuff ugly, make stuff that gets your message across however you can! Fancy is boring, perfect is dull, and nobody ever changed the world just because the thing they made was super shiny. You know the person you are, where your strengths lie, and what you're not as good at. You're not going to become an amazing drawer overnight if you're not one today—it doesn't matter. You're not going to magically become a mechanical engineer just because you figured out how to screw some boards together—you don't need to be. Because it doesn't matter: you are making a thing! And your passion can smooth the rough edges, mainly because you'll realize you're so into this thing you're making that you don't mind them so much.

What if I mess up?

OMG, you will. So many times! Messing up is part of the process. Is it frustrating? It sure is! But again: if you're not going to wait until you're an expert—and HOLY COW, don't—then you're going to mess up. That's just a fact of anything you're going to make no matter how long you make things for. Nothing springs forth fully formed like it jumped out of Zeus's skull. You're gonna have to be OK with messing up. And here's the big secret: messing up is how all of us learn. Making a mistake, figuring out what went wrong, correcting it and moving forward again: that's how you get better. We're always told that learning involves carefully following instructions, but that's just how you learn to follow instructions. It's when you end up in a weird corner you weren't expecting and need to find your way out of it that you really learn how to make something. Accept that messing up is going to happen and turn that frustration into a realization that you're gonna get better. Also, sometimes, put that thing you're making down and go on a walk—it helps.

What if I spend all this time making this thing and nobody cares?

Gonna be real on this one: whenever you make something, there's the possibility that nobody will care. I've made some stuff that a bunch of people have loved and I've made *way more things* that maybe reached a handful. First and foremost make that thing for *you* and then the rest doesn't matter. But also, when you're making things for a protest or an action and you bring it out into the world, you never know what will happen next. Someone's going to see it and that person is going to be moved one way or another. That's what's so magic about putting stuff out into the world: what that person does next is up to *them* and it may go in totally unexpected ways. But even if you move just that one person, you made an impact—hell, even if you

[114] MAUREEN JOHNSON

moved *yourself* you made an impact—and you put something out into the world that didn't exist before. You made something. You're amazing!

Making stuff is hard, but the hardest thing is the voices in your head telling you that you can't do it. Listen: we're our own worst critic; self-doubt is the hardest thing to overcome. Hopefully this advice will help quiet those voices a little bit—of course, as someone who's been making stuff since before you were born I'll tell you: they never go away entirely. Get out there and get making!

But before you go, there's a bigger thing, too: our world is so sanitized, finished, and clean that it's hard to remember that everything is made. Every part of your day is manufactured and designed—it's just designed for you not to notice. Making stuff, even when it's not for a protest, is a pretty radical act. When you learn to make stuff, you are subverting a culture that tries to remove the hand of people from the things around them. When you make stuff—even when it's not great or it's a rough draft or a first try—*you* are making things, too; you are designing your reality and starting to understand how everything comes together. Making stuff is subversive because it's the first step in knowing how to build a better world. Go!

Maya Rupert is an award-winning writer and activist who focuses on the intersection of race, gender, and culture. Her work has appeared in several outlets including The Atlantic, Slate, Salon, and O, the Oprah Magazine. She has been recognized by the National Association of Black Journalists for her writing and by national outlets like Ebony magazine and The Root for her leadership in the black community. She is the senior director of policy at the Center for Reproductive Rights and a Public Voices Fellow. Follow her on Twitter @MayaRupert.

I, WONDER: IMAGINING A BLACK WONDER WOMAN

Growing up, I was told that my favorite comic-book heroine was white. And yet her struggles always seemed uniquely similar to my own.

When I was eight years old, I asked my mother if Wonder Woman was black. It was 1989—almost thirty years before I'd eagerly await the premiere of the first *Wonder Woman* movie. As a child, I had seen the Amazonian princess portrayed by Lynda Carter, who looked unmistakably white, on the syndicated television show I loved. But in many iconic pictures in the comic books I read, Wonder Woman appeared to have a trace of melanin that made me think—maybe?

Maybe I could believably be her for Halloween? Or maybe, simply, I could be wonderful, too. "She's white," my mother told me, perhaps wistfully, but definitively. Not wanting to dash my hopes, she added, "But she's not real. So she can be whatever race you want her to be."

Later that week, at an after-school event, armed with a coloring book, a brown crayon, and my mother's voice still in my head, I filled in Wonder Woman's skin to match my own. A white mother who was supervising the students saw my work; with shock, she asked why I'd "ruined" my picture. I told her I'd wanted to make my heroine look like me. "It doesn't matter," the woman declared pointedly. "She doesn't have to look like you. You can still want to be her."

[118] MAUREEN JOHNSON

It seemed this sentiment was everywhere I turned at the time. "Race shouldn't matter," the late '80s had told me through the "very special episodes" of my favorite TV programs. From *Family Ties* to *The Golden Girls,* shows during this time tackled race and racism without ever acknowledging that racial differences mattered. These episodes were usually resolved with an appeal to commonalities and the message that racists were the only people who "saw color." According to popular culture of this era, gender differences were empowering, but racial differences were divisive. I didn't yet have a vocabulary that included "white feminism," a shorthand term for a "race-blind" form of feminism that ends up centering the needs of white women at the expense of women of color. Even so, I certainly had the model for it: I was allowed to prefer Wonder Woman to Superman, but I wasn't allowed to ask that Wonder Woman be black.

Comic books have long famously told stories of oppression—characters grapple with feelings of otherness and alienation, fear of discrimination, a need to hide a true identity. But so often these allegories center on super-powered individuals who are white and male, making their claim to these stories of marginalization ring false. Wonder Woman is white, I was reminded again and again. And yet, her story and overlapping identities—a superhero in a world of humans and a heroine in a world of heroes—felt uniquely familiar to me. They led me to think her character perhaps made more sense as a black woman.

Wonder Woman and I were both outsiders on two levels. Her powers set her apart from other humans, but among the other members of the Justice League, she was relegated to secretary. My race set me apart from my white classmates, but I learned at a young age that within the black community, my gender marked me as inferior. I remember as a child being told by my hairdresser that feminism wasn't for black women. "For us," she explained, "the man is here, and we're here," she said gesturing with her hands to illustrate that to be a black woman meant that a man I had never met would always be stationed above me. As I got older, I became better able to name my double displacement. I was frustrated with the racism I saw in feminist circles and with the misogyny I saw among racial-justice advocates. My awareness of this dynamic grew, and Wonder Woman's state of constant otherness only grew more meaningful.

But as a girl, I most commiserated with Wonder Woman when she sought to reconcile her inner strength and ferocity with the need of others to see her as peaceful and feminine. I had learned early on that it wouldn't take a lot for me to be viewed as angry and deemed unlikable. Images of neck-rolling, finger-snapping, gum-popping black women caricatured in movies and TV shows showed me exactly what people expected from me.

These expectations were memorably laid out by one of my favorite TV shows when I was ten, *Martin,* via two characters: Pam, the dark-skinned, needed-a-weave-to-hide-her-nappy-hair, perpetually single best friend; and Gina, the light-skinned, kind, and happy love interest. The jokes at Pam's expense came from the fact that she was supposedly too aggressive and masculine. Meanwhile, Gina, who clearly had a better role, was unabashedly feminine. I knew, with my dark skin, nappy hair, strong opinions, and sarcastic sense of humor that I'd be seen as a Pam. So over time, I became a bubbly, happy, slow-to-upset black girl you would never call angry. Even today, I wonder if the bubbly, happy, slow-to-upset black woman I've become is who I really am, or if it's just my own Diana Prince, the version of myself I created to protect my secret, real identity.

Wonder Woman seemed to understand this same psychic conflict. She's one of the strongest heroes in the DC Comics canon. According to one origin story, she was blessed with "the strength of Hercules," in the other, she's an actual demigoddess, the daughter of Zeus. Among comic-book fans, an ongoing debate rages over whether Wonder Woman could best Superman in a fight. But unlike her powerful peers, Wonder Woman must retain a femininity that her physical prowess seems to undermine. The result is

[120] MAUREEN JOHNSON

a sometimes-contradictory character—a warrior by training and birthright who prefers diplomacy to battle. A would-be Pam who was only ever supposed to be seen as Gina.

Wonder Woman once famously explained her philosophy: "We have a saying among my people. 'Don't kill if you can wound, don't wound if you can subdue, don't subdue if you can pacify. And don't raise your hand at all unless you've first extended it.'" It's a moving sentiment, but an odd one for a world in which one-dimensional villains often leave heroes with no other choice than violence. But perhaps not that odd after all, given that Wonder Woman's creator, William Moulten Marsten, was himself an imperfect feminist thinker who held the essentialist belief that women were naturally more peaceful than men.

Wonder Woman didn't get to act on anger, and neither did I. I was terrified of how I'd be seen if I ever did, in part because Wonder Woman once showed me exactly what could happen. In one famous storyline, *Sacrifice* part IV, Wonder Woman was forced to kill a villain, Maxwell Lord, to save Superman's and Batman's lives. Lord had tricked the Justice League members into thinking he was an ally, when in fact he planned to destroy all superheroes, whom he viewed as a global threat. Lord convinced Superman that both Batman and Wonder Woman were his enemies and forced him to attack. After subduing Batman, Superman came after Wonder Woman. Instead of fighting her friend, Wonder Woman captured Lord and used her Lasso of Truth. Lord told her the only way to stop him was to kill him. Which she did.

Unfortunately for Wonder Woman, that moment was broadcast publicly: the world saw Wonder Woman kill Lord without any context. The panel from that moment showed Wonder Woman from the perspective of those watching her, her face darkened and twisted into something ugly and murderous. The public turned on her. Even Superman and Batman, whose lives she had saved with her action, refused to hear her side and severed their friendship. This double standard infuriated me. This was nowhere near the first time a hero had killed in the service of a greater good. It wasn't her role as a hero that her actions betrayed, but her role as a woman. It was her loss of femininity, not the moral high ground that made this moment so shocking.

Wonder Woman's fate was one I had tried to avoid for years with a painful balancing act. Black women have long had to navigate stereotypes that create a similar sort of bind: our reputed preternatural strength is used as a weapon to force us to withstand greater physical, emotional, and spiritual burdens. The stereotype of the "strong black woman" becomes a self-fulfilling prophecy, and the identity of black women becomes indistinguishable from our struggle. This is evident in the archetype of the Mammy, the black maternal figure who acts as a cipher for the burdens of the white people around her and takes them on with an ever-present smile. In the '80s, she was Nell Carter, the happy maid to a white family on *Gimme A Break!,* and Florida Evans, the put-upon matriarch from *Good Times.* These women sublimated their own needs for those of others, and always did it with a smile.

But when black women stop smiling, as it were, they're easily reimagined as overly aggressive and mean. The Mammy archetype gives way to the Angry Black Woman trope, also known as Sapphire—named for the bullying black female character from the early American sitcom *The Amos 'n' Andy Show.* Sapphire's fury, and by extension the fury of black women, is assumed both to be an overreaction and inherently threatening. The result is that when a black woman shows anger, no matter how justified, she must immediately contend with the fear that her emotions will be seen, taken out of context, and result in everyone turning on her.

Wonder Woman, I felt, understood this impossible situation; I had seen her suffer for it. As I grew up, Wonder Woman grew with me. In later versions of her stories, her feminism became more self-aware and conscious

[122] MAUREEN JOHNSON

of the politics of the time in the same ways mine did. And as her symbolism for many female comic fans deepened, the special meaning she held for me deepened as well.

Since I found out the *Wonder Woman* movie was finally in the works, I've been excited but also a little nervous. Yes, a white actress, Gal Gadot, had been cast as the lead. But, I wondered, would the creators see in her what I had all these years? Would she still chafe at the forced dichotomy between her strength and her womanhood, her peaceful demeanor and her righteous anger? Would we still walk the same tightrope of dual identities and the resulting isolation from each? While all heroes won't be men, will all the Amazons be white? Would they infuse her story with enough of mine that a little black girl who sees the movie might get to wonder, maybe?

I'm sensitive to the argument that every character can't embody every identity, and that the solution to Hollywood's larger diversity problem can't possibly fall to any single movie or creator to fix. And yet I've begun to hear that argument not as a lament or a promise to do better with future characters and opportunities, but as a familiar admonishment to put away the brown crayon and stop trying to ruin the picture.

I have now seen *Wonder Woman* several times. I'll likely see it multiple times. And I'm sure I'll love it for many of the same reasons that I've been loving her since I was eight. But I'm also sure I'll keep challenging her to love me a little more. I've been doing that since I was eight, too.

ROSIE O'DONNELL

Rosie O'Donnell is an activist, comedian, actress, and author best known for her starring roles on the Emmy Award–winning talk shows The Rosie O'Donnell Show and The View. She has long been committed to LGBTQ rights activism and launched her own charity, Rosie's Theater Kids, to help children discover their greatness through the power of music, dance, and drama. She has also been a magazine editor and continues to be a television producer, lesbian rights activist, celebrity blogger, and collaborative partner in the LGBT family vacation company, R Family Vacations. Follow her on Twitter @Rosie.

ROSIE O'DONNELL'S FIVE RESISTANCE STEPS

1. learn everything u can

2. find like-minded folk

3. use ur voice

4. tweet ur ass off

● ● ●

5. show up

Jacqueline Woodson's awards include four Newbery Honors, two Coretta Scott King Awards and three Coretta Scott King Honors, a National Book Award and three National Book Award Finalists, a Margaret A. Edwards Award and an ALAN Award—both for Lifetime Achievement in YA Literature. She is the former Young People's Poet Laureate and lives with her family in Brooklyn, New York.

Where were you the first time you felt called to resist?

JACQUELINE: Wow. My earliest memory is watching *The Brady Bunch* as a child, and not seeing any reflection of myself. I just remember the sheer recognition of my absence, and being really angry about that. And already knowing that that lack of reflection of myself in the world was wrong. And something that I'd have to fight against.

Where were you at the time?

JACQUELINE: I was living in Brooklyn, in this community that was predominantly black and Latino, and I saw myself everywhere. And having *The Brady Bunch,* and falling in love with this show at nine and ten, but knowing there was a resistance to me, led to a kind of counterresistance, I guess.

I didn't know how I'd write myself into a narrative like that, but I knew I'd have to do something.

[130] MAUREEN JOHNSON

Was your writing a direct answer to not being seen?

JACQUELINE: Definitely. It was the sheer audacity of a country to not see me and people who look like me. At the same time I was growing up, there was Shirley Chisholm, Angela Davis, and the Black Power Movement. So I was growing up in a circle of resistance. The Civil Rights movement was at my back door, so it wasn't even a question of not acting. Or not reacting. It was just what you did when things weren't right. I definitely felt it from a very young age, because in the world there was invisibility.

Has it gotten better?

JACQUELINE: Somewhat, in mainstream media. For me, I don't watch much TV. (*Laughs.*) My partner and I kind of control as much as we can, so our family movie night is *black-ish*. Our community is very mixed families—Korean, Scottish, Irish. My partner's Jewish, the kids are biracial. The world they're moving in is a very mixed community.

So when kids don't "get" race my son is appalled. My son is like, what's the question, around transgender folks.

But now my daughter is fifteen and can stream what she wants. At one point she was very into the TV show *Friends*. But she has this narrative: the show is messed up, because of race politics, but I'll take my entertainment. But she understands. There isn't enough representation on TV. They still don't see a lot of mirrors for themselves.

Where do you find hope, now?

JACQUELINE: I find it in young people. I just wish I could channel the energy and passion and compartmentalizing that young people are able to do, to erase the moment. I ask my daughter: how do you find hope now? And she was like: what's going on—in terms of politics and healthcare and women's rights—that's not everything to us. We've got Snapchat, our friends; are we going to get into good colleges? And go to that party Saturday? We're trying to live full lives. For me, I can sit and spin in a moment. There are so many negative moments. So I turn to the young people and have conversations; they know about climate change but they don't see it being the end of their lifetime. And for us as we get older, and look to our own mortality, we do an external gaze of our lifetime. But our kids are like, this isn't the end of our lifetime. We're just beginning.

How does a kid with little access start resisting today?

JACQUELINE: Ya know, the main thing is—Audre Lorde said, "We can sit in our safe corners mute as bottles and we will still be no less afraid." There is so much fear-mongering. People think it's easier to be silent. To tiptoe around stuff, as opposed to having conversations and confronting and disrupting.

Especially for young people—fear eats you from the inside out. So the way to live a life is to live it fully and to know you have the right no matter who you are to walk through the world. And once you deeply understand that, it's easier to call into question people who are being phobic, misogynistic. It's easier to begin that conversation.

[132] MAUREEN JOHNSON

I was having this conversation with my son and his nephew. He lives in a different world. He was saying he didn't want to touch something. He made some anti-gay comment. And I said, you know this is a queer family, right? And he said lesbian is different than gay. And I say: there's no tolerance for any kind of homophobia here. And he said, I heard it from another kid in camp. And so my partner and I started to explain how important it is to be an ally, even if you aren't the queer child, for the people who don't have the voice.

We see the signs that say LOVE TRUMPS HATE, and I think that is a way to approach something. It's gently. And has a dynamic impact. The minute you say to someone, "You're racist," they shut down. You have to say "I" in a relationship. "I'm hurt by this comment."

What's something you would tell your younger self about the future?

JACQUELINE: Living in this moment is a moment I never imagined, but always knew was coming. I don't know how to explain that. I would tell my younger self about fear. And say: fear doesn't move us forward, it's what keeps us where we are. My younger self was a bit of a mess. I would say, you have every right to walk through the world safely. And take action if someone is not allowing you to do that. There were times I didn't think I had a right to be safe. Look, I was at Studio 54 at fourteen. You have to unlearn the self-blaming.

Libba Bray is the #1 New York Times bestselling author of the Gemma Doyle trilogy (A Great and Terrible Beauty, Rebel Angels, The Sweet Far Thing); *the Michael L. Printz Award–winning* Going Bovine; Beauty Queens, *a Los Angeles Times Book Prize finalist; and The Diviners series. She lives in New York City. You can find Libba at www.libbabray.com, on Twitter @libbabray, and Instagram @libbabray.*

AN ANNOUNCEMENT FROM MUFFY HIGGINBOTTOM, PRESIDENT OF DELTA SIGMA TAU SORORITY RESISTANCE COMMITTEE

Good morning, Resisters.

Thank you for coming downstairs before noon. Ji-Won and Oksana: I know you were up waayyyy late making sure that Ruth Bader Ginsburg's Delta Sigma Tau–designed oxygen chamber didn't spring a leak, so big ups to y'all. It is our mission to keep the RBG alive for the next four years. I don't think I have to impress upon you the importance of this.

I'd like to start with some XXL snaps to our Grrrrilla Merch™ team—Aisha, Polly, Deepika, and Max—for the awesome new resistance products. In addition to the ever-popular "My Lady Business Is None of Yours" T-shirts, we also have the "Make America Stop Being Such an Asshole" hats, "Keep Your Laws Off My Gender Fluids" hoodies, and my personal favorite, the Delta Sigma Tau swimsuits with a shark crotch and the tag, "Grab at your own risk." All proceeds will fund our new women's healthcare van, The Cervehicle™. The Cervehicle™ will deliver free feminine hygiene, Pap smears, and sex ed classes to an America that still thinks that every time insurance covers a woman's Pap smear, the terrorists win. There's an "us" in uterus, sisters. Let's roll. (Thanks, Achutebe, Nahla, Esther,

[136] MAUREEN JOHNSON

Jennifer, and Jennifer for coming up with the alternate name, the Roving Ovaries™, and more snaps to our med team on bikes: the Reproductive Cycles™.)

These are dark days, resisters. As bitchin' babes of Delta Sigma Tau, much is asked of us if we don't want to see reason, facts, rights, civility, and democracy replaced by a government that's like WWF-meets-Kafka with a loop of Mel Brooks pleading, "But I was kidding! KIDDING!" Resistance work can feel overwhelming at times: What to do? Where to start? How to keep going?

My fellow resisters, there's a lot to fight these days, and you can't be everywhere. You're not Jesus. Or a Kardashian.

So today, I want to talk about the importance of a small act of resistance that you can pass on to others. I'm talking about the importance of educating yourselves through reading, and about sourcing that reading to find out whether it came from a reputable outfit or was cooked up in an information meth-lab by paranoid, three-toothed internet trolls during masturbation breaks.

Some of you have asked, "Muffy, how can we be sure that what we're reading isn't 'fake news'?" That is an excellent question! Almost as excellent as, "Who borrowed my diaphragm?" (Mirwat: I appreciate your feminist modern art collage, but, seriously—I have a need. Return, please? Thanks.) Real journalists have to abide by a journalistic code of ethics. They have a staff of fact-checkers. They can provide documentation for their reporting, and if they get something wrong in a story, they have to issue a correction or retraction. They don't respond to every challenge with a huffy, "Your mama!" Real, objective news outlets are places like *The New Yorker, The Washington Post,* Reuters, the Associated Press, *Time* magazine, and *Teen Vogue.*

Real journalism trades in facts. Facts are not the same thing as opinions. Opinions are things like, "*Star Wars* would be a thousand times better acted out by meerkats." Opinions are the speaker's thoughts and feelings and, occasionally, a glimpse of the abyss. "I, the speaker, have strong feelings about both *Star Wars* and meerkats" is a belief. Doesn't make it true. Facts, on the other hand, can be verified through evidence—a reporter's notes, for example, or through scientific observation; collected data; scholarly, peer-reviewed analysis; standards of law; or historical record. Facts stand up to scrutiny and challenge. Facts matter, my fellow resisters. They matter if we're not going to live in a nation where healthcare has been replaced by Facebook prayer circles and homemade aspirin, where children eat pencil lead and tubes of Crest because there's no funding for school lunches anymore, and people believe that the Revolutionary War was fought with Mexico over a border wall.

What I'm saying to you, resisters, is that it's super, super important to read but also to find out where that reading material is coming from and who might have an agenda or bias behind it.

Now. I want to tell you a personal story about my aunt Zippee that proves this point.

Just last week, I went home to Bogswamp, Texas, for the Higginbottom family reunion. (Sidebar: Anybody got some spare Xanax? I used all mine to spike my uncle Bubba's sweet tea. Judge me if you like, but it's an open-carry state, y'all, and I wasn't taking any chances.) My great-aunt Zippee showed up to the BBQ wearing a MAGA muumuu that reimagined Pence, McConnell, Ryan, and 45 as Mount Rushmore. Unfortunately, the dress had been run off in the local print shop—"Guns, God, and Garments"—so the image was upside down, which put Mitch McConnell's dying turtle mouth right over Aunt Zippee's Precious Portal. On the plus side, I'm pretty sure it's the closest Pence has been to some lady parts in a while.

"How do you like my outfit?" Aunt Zippee asked, giving the muumuu a good twirl.

I was grateful for the breeze.

[138] MAUREEN JOHNSON

"Are you sure Mike Pence is allowed to be alone near your left rib?" I said. "What if he accidentally makes a woman out of it? Also . . . is that Pence's head on Justin Bieber's body?"

"That's not Justin Bieber! Our vice president is ripped hard! Making America great again gives you big muscles that you can use to carry your sword of Righteous Tax Cuts. At least you can in Texas, where God wants you to be able to kill everybody without government regulations."

"Aunt Zippee, that is literally Justin Bieber's body. I recognize the 'Selena Sux' tattoo next to the big cross."

"Lots of people have that."

Long story short: before she dug into her fried catfish, Aunt Zippee started telling me that there's a secret liberal storehouse of alien blood smoothies that all "lamestream media newsfolk" drink: "They're just a front for the alien overlords that want to come in and destroy our country, take our guns, and force us to put lipstick on all our Jesus mantel paintings."

"Mmhmm. Aunt Zip, where'd you get that info?" I asked this while also moving the cutlery out of the way because, hello!

"Oh! It's on this website, LizardPeepleR4Real@KremlinCutie.com."

"Aunt Zippee, you know that website's run by a cult of Koch brother–funded moon-landing deniers who, on the regular, perform a reenactment of earth's beginnings where God rides into Mordor on the back of a *T. rex* singing Toby Keith songs? It's in the public record."

She patted her beehive. "Well. I like Toby Keith. Those *T. rex* have good taste."

Now, Aunt Zippee once had to go to rehab for inhaling Downy Fabric Softener straight from the bottle. She'd huff up some Spring Garden goodness while watching the Miss Universe Pageant and eating Winn-Dixie orange sherbet. So, in a way, Aunt Zip's been living the Trump presidency for a long time. But Aunt Zippee demonstrates what happens when you abdicate your responsibility to educate yourself and just suck up crazy opinions-masquerading-as-news like you would a bag of Nacho Cheese Doritos at two a.m. I admit that once upon a time, I loved me some conspiracy theories. I wanted all those far-out things I heard to be true. Like at a sleepover, when Ashleigh Juggins told me that *The Omen* was based on a true story and that Damien the Antichrist had enrolled at Bogswamp High, I was stoked. I hoped that Damien-Not-Jesus was hot. It gave my life meaning. Most importantly, I had somebody to blame when everything felt out of my control—I didn't fail that math quiz; the secret Antichrist of Bogswamp High made me fail!

Sometimes, it's easier to go down a rabbit hole of absurdity rather than take responsibility for your own fact-checking.

But here's the thing: this moment in America didn't just happen overnight, y'all. I'm sorry to say that, like my cousin Ray-Bob and public nuisance arrests, America has a bit of a record. It's important to know our nation's history, and not just the warm and fuzzy bits, so you don't get duped by the world's worst blood-gargling metal band of orange-faced demagogues playing the same old, tired set list of industrial noise, calling it America's Greatest Hits, and trying to convince you it is sweet, sweet music. Read the Constitution. Read the Bill of Rights. Read history. Our full history. That thing I said about bias? It exists there, too. So educate yourselves about facts like Jim Crow. The Chinese Exclusion Act. The Trail of Tears. Read about our habit of nativism and xenophobia. Read for facts but read also for context and understanding. Read backward in order to move forward, resisters.

The best part? You can find everything you need at your local library. Libraries: serving the resistance since forever. Seriously, libraries are The. Best. Don't even bother fighting me on this one. You will lose.

You know what, y'all? Just read everything: Newspapers. Books. Comics. Plays. Satire. (Satire is what we used to have for outrageous, good-times laughs before reality started dropping acid on us, and it felt as if we were all

[140] MAUREEN JOHNSON

working the triage unit of the Reality Tripping Tent at some alt-universe Presidential Coachella. Seriously: Sometimes I'm not convinced Kellyanne Conway isn't a hallucination left over from the time I took three Motrin for bad cramps at Bible sleep-away camp and kept whispering, "Shh, I am a pillar of salt. Keep running . . .")

Reading is Resistance. That's an opinion, but if you want the facts, read for yourselves.

Okay, y'all. There's a lot to do, so let's get to work. We at Delta Sigma Tau are your sisters in this. We are your ReSisters. We got you; you got this.

And if you see us out in the Cervehicle™, come say hi. Bonus: free birth control.

Yours in Resistance,
Muffy Higginbottom
President

(Maybe for real one day. Fingers crossed.)

Jonathan Sun is the author behind @jonnysun and Everyone's a Aliebn When Ur a Aliebn Too (HarperPerennial, 2017). He is currently a doctoral student at MIT, an affiliate at the Berkman Klein Center for Internet & Society at Harvard, and a creative researcher at the Harvard metaLAB, where he studies social media and online community. He is also a playwright, artist, illustrator, and previously studied as an architect and engineer. He is the creator of @tinycarebot, and his comedic work has appeared on NPR and in McSweeney's. In 2017, he was named one of Time magazine's 25 Most Influential People on the Internet.

MEDIA-CONSCIOUSNESS AS PART OF RESISTANCE!

Media exists because people will it into the world. It is conscious and active. It is important to think about media when thinking about resistance because **media works by shaping what we see, and how we see it.**

I often spend time wondering how I have come to my understanding of the world, and where I have gotten all my views, ideas, and biases from. Some of this is a combination of my own experiences and the experiences of others as they are directly passed on to me. These are things that shape me directly: through personal relationships, shared in one-on-one conversations, or from within small groups. But media is something else, and does something else.

Media is created and then transmitted, distributed, or shared in one direction, along a platform for mass communication, from a source to an audience. Media is fundamentally different than a one-on-one experience being shared between you and someone else: a friend, a family member. Media is a piece of information broadcast from one to many. The methods of mass communication, the ways of spreading media these days, are vast and diverse. There is what is now "traditional" media: TV, film, radio, newspapers. There is what we call "new" media—the internet, and all it encompasses, lately: YouTube, Facebook, Twitter, Instagram, Snapchat, Vine (RIP). Increasingly, we spend more and more time on social media, and therefore get more and more of our media from these online platforms.

[144] MAUREEN JOHNSON

By being shared on all platforms of mass viewership, media is essentially what we all—as a culture and a society—see. In a way, media purports to be what we all—as "the general public"—believe, too. This is, or should be, a little troubling. Media dictates our norms, our culture. It dictates what we as a collective society should think is important and where to focus our attention on. It decides what, to an extent, is "real" in our world, what values are "true," what biases are "fact." This is especially troubling when we understand that media is not created *by* its mass viewers; rather, it is created *for* a mass viewership. Because it's everywhere, and so ubiquitous in our lives, media has an enormous amount of control over the way we think and the way we see the world.

Social media may be a space where we as viewers have more agency. Whereas "traditional" media (TV, film, and the like) runs on a hierarchical system, with plenty of gatekeepers and Old Rich People in power and control, perhaps social media can be different. Perhaps here, on social media, on the internet, we don't have to rely on the gatekeepers of traditional media to determine what should be represented and how it should be represented. Work created on social media is a step toward a greater range of voices all over, and I believe that all of us, not as creators but as viewers and consumers, have power in this equation. Social media is far from perfect, but it's perhaps a more direct form of media (and it's dangerous for this same reason, too). It's also powerful in the sense that it is for so many of us our default place where we spend our time, where we see things, where we get our news and entertainment from.

Social media is different from traditional media, too, in the sense that we, as viewers, as followers, as users, play a more active role in the ability for media to get distributed. We play this role by actively sharing, retweeting, liking, reblogging. Each of those becomes a "vote" that this is what we believe is important to be shared; that this is the viewpoint, the opinion, the art, that we stand for. And each share literally spreads the media one

HOW I RESIST [145]

more link down the chain. The fact that we are able to actively share media through retweeting means we have a more active role in helping good things get seen.

Media is not inherently good or bad—it is the product of those who create it and how we see it. But it is inherently active. The better we are at understanding that all media is a conscious act of creation, and understanding that we as viewers and *sharers* play an active role in spreading certain viewpoints and voices, the better we can get understanding media's role, and our role, in shaping our views on the world.

In the past few years, I've become more and more aware of my role not as a creator or a writer, but as a viewer and as a sharer. I wanted to share with you the questions I try to ask myself when looking at media, both online and off, in an effort to try to consume and share media more positively and constructively. As viewers, resistance begins with us! Together, we can create a more conscious media ecosystem!

Jonny's notes for consuming and reacting to media!*

10 THINGS TO THINK ABOUT WHEN CONSUMING MEDIA:

1. Who created the work? And why?

Every piece of media has an author (or a group of authors). We need to think about who the author is, what their intentions were behind creating

---

* I want to stress that this is just as important when looking at anything from traditional "big" media down to anything you see on social media! This is also in no way complete—but they are my current working notes when I spend all day online, and hope they help you. I fully expect these questions to morph and grow and change as our world and our media change. I know this is a lot to keep in mind when looking at memes all day, but memes are media, too! And they shape our perspectives and worldviews. It's important to think about this stuff! Also, I made these listicles so they'd be easier to go through.

the work, if they are informed enough to contribute to the discourse that the work is part of, the message behind the work, and how the politics of the author influence or appear within the work.

2. What is the underlying message of the piece of media?

Sometimes it's difficult to spot the takeaway message. Often, messages either reinforce or try to combat norms and biases. They hold worldviews and opinions of "how the world is" or "how the world should be." For me, I often try to get to the heart of it by completing a sentence like: "It's funny because . . ." or "It's sad because . . ." or "It's inspiring because . . ." This may help.

3. What assumptions do you and the author have to agree on to understand this piece of media?

In engaging with media, it's helpful, too, to think about where your own worldviews and the worldviews of the work align or conflict. This should create an internal dialogue between yourself and the piece. I ask myself how I react to the work and think about why I respond to it the way that I do— which parts of my own worldviews react to the worldviews of the piece. I think about what the author is trying to say, and if they achieve that. And when you do identify it, is the message constructive? Is it toxic? Does it normalize biases or toxic worldviews? If it's funny—*why* is it funny?—and what do you have to agree with in the joke for it to be funny to you? Do you agree with it? Why or why not? What do you wish to learn from the piece, or what do you wish not to learn from the piece? Does this viewpoint reinforce your existing viewpoints? Can you find ones that expand or challenge your viewpoints?

4. Where did this piece of media come from? Who is distributing the work? What is the motive of the distributor to distribute this work?

Just as there is an author to every piece of media, there is also a distributor, someone who shares the piece so that you see it. In traditional media, this may be a network, a studio, a channel. In social media or online media, this may be a crowd, your friends, a celebrity, a content aggregator. Just as an author has a specific message they want to embed in the piece, distributors have reasons for sharing the piece, too. Is it to generate views and clicks? Is it to appeal to a certain group of people—and if so, why? Is it to generate controversy? Is it to signal that they align with the message in the piece? Asking questions like these help to understand why certain media gets shared and why it may go viral—the intentions for sharing may not always be clear or pure.

5. Does the piece of media *tell* a truth or *sell* a truth?

That is, is the work authentic and honest? Are the authors of the work able to make the work honest—or are they "qualified" to create this piece? Is the work telling a truth about the world? Or is the work trying to sell you on a message that may not be true about the world? Is it manipulating you into believing something? All media is emotionally manipulative by nature— but trying to get to the underlying intention of that manipulation is important. Does it manipulate you into empathizing with a truth you wouldn't otherwise be aware of? Or does it manipulate you into buying a lie? What is truth anyway? What is your truth?

[148] MAUREEN JOHNSON

6. Does the media come from a perspective that is different from your own?

What can you learn from it? Or, what do you actively wish to refute from it? Which perspectives are you missing from your own worldview that would help to learn from and understand? Which perspectives are harmful against others, are used by those in power to oppress?

7. Does the piece of media confirm existing stereotypes? Does it upend them? Does it upend them without relying on other stereotypes?

Stereotypes have existed forever as "shortcuts" to bigotry and oppression. They say, "We didn't want to—or we weren't able to—put in the time and effort to understand a whole group of people, so instead here are some sweeping generalizations that allow us to feel better about not putting in the time and effort to get to know members of that group." Stereotypes are bred from willful ignorance and malicious intent. In media, reinforcing biases and stereotypes become dangerous and harmful. Does this piece of media play into this? Does it avoid it without playing into other stereotypes? Is the piece taking the time to tell honest, complicated, complex stories?

8. Is the creator someone who might not have been given access to a creative voice and platform traditionally?

One power of social media is the emergence of traditionally underrepresented voices and perspectives. While far from perfect, we are gradually being able to hear from more and more different voices, different artists, coming from different experiences and worldviews. Does the piece of media come from new perspectives? Or does it come from existing ones? In this way, does it reinforce existing perspectives within media, or does it introduce new ones? And, are these new perspectives constructive ones that deserve a platform, or harmful ones that don't?

9. Is the piece of media original? Is it derivative? Is it stolen?

In traditional and new media, there is a lot of profit to be made from taking the work of others. Usually, this is in the form of taking the work of already marginalized or underrepresented voices. The ones who benefit from stealing the works of others are those already in positions of power, or those with enough privilege to do this and not face consequences. The ones being stolen from are those without (or perceived to be without) enough of a voice or platform to call them out on it in any way that will impact the aggressor. Stealing takes many forms. It can be direct plagiarism—someone lifting someone else's work and claiming it as their own. It can be derivative—someone, instead of sharing the work and celebrating the original, decides they want the credit or profit from it and creates something very similar, profiting from the work of the original. If the piece of media you see has been taken from another source, can you find (and share) the original source instead?

10. Is this media harmful?

Ultimately, we need to ask if the piece of media is harmful, if it's toxic, if it propagates stereotypes, if it is being used to hurt or oppress. Some of this is blatant (and increasingly, harmful media is *shockingly* blatant). Some of this is more hidden and, in a way, more dangerous.

[150] MAUREEN JOHNSON

6 WAYS TO REACT TO MEDIA:

1. Call out BS, engage in media, have tough conversations.

Make your voice heard—it is one of the most important tools you have.

2. But also . . . realize when it's not your turn to talk.

We are going through a time of Extreme Discourse. When your voice has power, use it. But also recognize when it is more constructive to listen, to sit back, to learn. Make room for people with constructive and relevant experiences and perspectives to share them. Sometimes, making room for this looks like not saying anything yourself, or taking a step back. Don't mistake this as passive—this is an active step, too, when done consciously.

3. Think about what media, and from what perspectives, you are not seeing—and see if there are ways to find it and share it.

Usually, this means looking for media being created by people who are traditionally erased or underrepresented in media. When you do find more work created by marginalized voices, what can you do to help support, share, and amplify their voices?

4. Share and engage in work you believe in.

Ultimately, your power as a viewer—especially in social media—comes from being part of a vast network of people spreading media across the internet. Sharing and engaging is an active part of social media today. By doing so, you are helping voices get heard, you are helping combat existing norms and introducing your world and your networks to new perspectives. Every little bit counts.

5. Create your own work!

Finally, when you are ready, make your own work! Make your voice heard! Create what only you, with your unique sets of experiences, worldviews, and perspectives, can make! All the points I've listed here are necessary for consuming and sharing media responsibly, but are also necessary to think of when creating media responsibly, too.

6. Recognize media has the power to create change.

Whether you are sharing media or creating it, the point I want to drive home the most is that media is powerful. Media exists constantly, in the background of all of our lives. It slowly shapes our narratives, it slowly sets our norms. To make change, to resist, we need to have the immediate and direct forms of resistance, but we also need to play the long game. Resisting through media is one way to influence the background, the underlying perspectives and worldviews in our lives. This, in turn, helps bring change to the foreground, and helps guide what we all choose to do here on this earth.

Thanks for listening.

Jodi Picoult is the author of twenty-four novels, with forty million copies sold worldwide. Her last ten books have debuted at #1 on the New York Times Best Seller List, including the recent Small Great Things. Five novels have been made into movies and Between the Lines (cowritten with daughter Samantha van Leer) has been adapted as a musical. She is the recipient of multiple awards, including the Alex Award from the YA Library Services Association, and the NH Literary Award for outstanding literary merit. She lives in New Hampshire with her husband. Find her at www.jodipicoult.com, @jodipicoult (Instagram/Twitter), and at www.facebook.com/jodipicoult/.

Not too long ago, I had a very heated argument with a very famous person who shall remain anonymous. One of my YA novels, *Between the Lines,* was being adapted as a Broadway-bound musical, and the Very Famous Person had read a recent version of the script. "It just feels . . . too political," he said.

I stared at him. "What is the point of art if it's *not* political?" I asked.

One of the great gifts of theater, fiction, and visual art is the message couched in the medium. People think they are coming to it as a form of entertainment and then, almost accidentally, wind up thinking about the contentious and thorny issues raised. Racism, sexism, ableism, women's rights, gay rights—every single one of those is at the heart of the stories we tell. That's why we tell them, right? So that people without a voice have a chance to be heard.

That seems to be a recurring theme in the current political administration—the systematic stripping away of voices. Whether it's removing the mention of LGBT people from a government website or literally separating undocumented immigrants from their families to deport them—there is a growing, loud chorus of majority that is attempting to drown out the rest of us.

I was in Australia during the election. I have never felt so isolated in my life. A friend in the U.S. stayed awake, texting me the results. Numb, I went out to dinner with a colleague only to hear some Aussies at the next table

[156] MAUREEN JOHNSON

making fun of America, which had been stupid enough to elect a buffoon. I found myself standing up, shaking. I stared at them. "What you're making fun of," I said, "is actually going to be devastating to people I know. I have friends and family who will live in fear of being killed in a hate crime; of being fired for their sexual orientation. What's a joke to you is very, very real to me."

They shut up.

It sounds silly, but the beginning of resistance is *resist*. It is not just enough to stay in a liberal social media bubble, commiserating with your friends about how long it is until the 2018 election. It's not enough to walk around in a fog wondering how an individual can make a difference. You need to get out and raise your voice.

That takes multiple forms. You can march, as I have—keynoting the satellite Women's March in New Hampshire. But I have also spent countless hours trying to talk individually to people who think differently from me. Who believe that the policies of the current administration will help, not hurt, most Americans. Look, it's easier to just shake your head and walk away from that confrontation. But if someone is willing to talk to me (not shout, but talk) then I feel like it is my obligation to do the same. I share the same personal stories with him or her. Sometimes I change their mind. Sometimes I don't. But I try.

What changes minds, I have found, are not statistics, but human beings. Gay rights and women's health are pretty vague issues until you meet someone who was forced to go to a conversion camp in Georgia, or a woman who had to terminate a pregnancy because she couldn't afford another child. I've shared stories of my son Jake's congenital preexisting condition and the thirteen surgeries he had as a result, and how without health coverage, we would have been bankrupt. I've brought my other son Kyle and his husband Kevin to events, so that they can see that fighting for gay marriage and gay rights is not just important to me, but that the results are incredibly beautiful. I talk about states like Alabama that just passed a law that allows gay couples to be discriminated against for adoption. Should Kyle's future be determined by his zip code?

What matters to you the most, and why does it matter? What rights are you worried about losing, or whose lives do you fear for? Tell their stories.

Maybe you will tell them in a school newspaper. Maybe you will join a rally and be courageous enough to speak. Maybe you will encourage your drama department to perform *The Laramie Project*. Maybe you'll start a reading group, and talk about *The Handmaid's Tale*. Maybe you will stand on a corner in your town with a BLACK LIVES MATTER sign. And here's the amazing thing: if you stand up and do it, someone else will. And two voices are louder than one. And so on . . . and so on.

Historically, Americans are very good at resisting. I keep clinging to that fact, and I remember that this country began when a bunch of ragtag citizens decided it was time to stand up to a bully. I also triumph in the fact that we live in a time when news travels lightning-fast, and because of that, we can organize. We aren't fighting in a vacuum, and we aren't alone, even when it sometimes feels that way. I also know that it's your generation, not mine, that's going to bring a climate of acceptance and respect to this country. I'm grateful that you are the future.

I used to believe that it was my generation's job to teach the next generation how to create equitable paths to success irrespective of gender, sex, race, physical ability. Now I am rethinking that. I believe it is the younger generation's job to school the older one. To hold society—and the president— accountable every time a woman is reduced to her appearance. Speak out when you see that happening. Even if it means standing up to an authority figure, like a boss—or a president. Go out of your way to compliment a woman—not on how great she looks in a pair of tight jeans, but for how insightful she is about a particular issue. If you see a girl in class or at a job being objectified, or having some guy mansplain to them, interrupt. If you

[158] MAUREEN JOHNSON

are a woman yourself, do it out of solidarity, in the hopes that one day some-one else might stand with you. If you are not a woman, do it because you wouldn't be here without one.

This is a singular moment in history, where young people actually seem to know more than their elders, and, perhaps, the president. You know, for example, that a person's character matters more than their gender. You know that those who are truly powerful don't punch down—they lift others up.

I'm still doing my part. My last book was about racism. My upcoming book is about what happens when you restrict abortion rights.

And that musical adaptation? Oh, I made a few of the changes the Very Famous Person wanted. But then I gave that character the best soliloquy in the show—one that calls out homophobia and anti-LGBT legislation and is very, very political.

Mark my words: it's gonna get a standing ovation.

KATE LINNEA WELSH

Kate Linnea Welsh is a writer and spreadsheet enthusiast who lives in New Hampshire. She got involved in political activism because the stress of living in a swing state that also has the earliest primary was keeping her up at night. Follow her on Twitter and Instagram @katelinnea, and read her commentary and daily curated link digests at www.katelinneawelsh.com.

THREE EASY STEPS TO CONTACT YOUR REPS

All fired up and ready to get in touch with the politicians representing YOU? Here are three easy steps to make it happen:

Step One: Pick your issue. There are a lot of important ones (health care! immigration! voting rights!), and it's easy to get overwhelmed. Pick one thing that's important to you to focus on right now.

Step Two: Find your elected official. For **national** issues, like the country's refugee policies, contact your U.S. senator or representative.

For **state** issues, like voter ID laws, contact your governor or state senator or representative.

For **local** issues, like school budgets and policies, contact the officials in your city or town: mayor, city council, aldermen, selectmen, whatever you have!

Don't know where to find them? Start here: https://www.usa.gov/elected -officials, or just go online and search: "How to get in touch with my reps."

[162] MAUREEN JOHNSON

Step Three: Communicate! Not sure what to say? Just fill in the blanks and email (or snail mail) away!

Dear _____ [their full name],

My name is _____ [your full name] and I am a __ [age]-year-old constituent who lives in _____ [place]. I am writing to you as my _____ [their position] to express my views on _____ [issue]. This is important to me because _____ [your reasons]. I urge you to _____ [what you want them to do: Vote for or against something? Fund a program? Do some research and reconsider their position?]. Thank you for your time and consideration.

Sincerely,

_____ [your name]
_____ [your address, if it's okay with your parents; otherwise, just your hometown is fine]

Congratulations! You're now an engaged citizen and part of the democratic process!

ALEX GINO

Alex Gino loves glitter, ice cream, gardening, awe-ful puns, and stories that reflect the diversity and complexity of being alive. They would take a quiet coffee date with a friend over a loud and crowded party any day. Born and raised on Staten Island, New York, Alex has lived in Philadelphia, Pennsylvania; Brooklyn, New York; Astoria (Queens), New York; and Northampton, Massachusetts; and now lives in Oakland, California. Their first book, George, won Stonewall and Lambda Literary Awards. Their second middle grade novel, You Don't Know Everything, Jilly P!, features a hearing white girl learning about ableism, racism, police violence, privilege, and mistakes.

Resistance is disruption. Resistance is yelling. Resistance is being in the streets and the council meetings and all the places where your presence declares your opposition. Resistance is making phone calls. Resistance is donating your money and time. Resistance is meetings that last long into the evening and art builds that last long into the night.

At least, that is the face of resistance. And all of it is needed today as much as ever, to counter conservatives who fear a changing society and are grasping onto old racisms and sexisms with emboldened ferocity. But gosh, it sounds tiring.

And what's more, the face is all it is. It's the visible part, the part people think of when they think of The Resistance. But that type of resistance surges and fades easily, because it is exhausting without a deeper resistance sustaining it. The Resistance of people sharing our stories and listening to the stories of others. The Resistance of being connected humans with empathy and love. The Resistance of building community in the face of institutions that want us to be individual consumers living isolated lives.

As a young feminist, I learned that the personal is political. I didn't really know what it meant, but I figured it had something to do with thinking bigger about what's "important." It's a phrase that I've connected with for a

[166] MAUREEN JOHNSON

long time, but I didn't realize just how deeply until a few weeks ago, when I read Carol Hanisch's 1969 essay, "The Personal Is Political."*

Okay, bear with me for a bit as I get into some history and theory. Hanisch wrote her essay in defense of meetings where women gathered to talk about their daily struggles and to find connections between their stories. Opponents called the meetings "therapy," but they were not about healing people (though that would have been valid). Instead, these women were engaging in two distinguished human skills: communication and problem-solving. As the people in these groups told their stories, they found the same issues rising again and again, though each person toiled as if they were the only one.

Hanisch and others learned that "There are no personal solutions at this time. There is only collective action for a collective solution." A hundred thousand fights over housework based on gender roles weren't a hundred thousand personal problems, they were (and are) part of a much larger, systemic problem that requires connection and interdependence to solve. They were Consciousness Raising, which is second-wave feminist for Getting Woke.

So what does an essay about the political climate fifty years ago steeped in white feminism have to do with how I resist today? A lot, it turns out.

Feeling alone in times of political crisis is overwhelming. It's also extremely common, and it can be debilitating. Sure, you can call your senators and write your representatives—and you should—but it can feel like screaming into the wind. And at some level, it is. One phone call rarely changes a congressperson's mind. Nor does a solitary vote in a national election. Nor does a single raindrop in a hurricane. And so doing it indi-

---

* Hanisch's essay is available on the internet. It's a thoughtful read and an interesting slice of feminist history. It's only about 1,750 words, but note that it is rooted in second-wave white feminism and is woefully non-intersectional. For example, Hanisch refers to "women, blacks, and workers" several times, but never once mentions Black working women.

vidually feels like it's nothing. But it's larger than one vote, or even one election. It's connecting yourself to a community that makes decisions collectively.

When you talk about your activism, you're likely to do more, and the people you talk with might be motivated to get more engaged as well. But it's not just about getting people to act. The connection itself is key to resistance. The more connected we are, the more unbreakable we are. The more we communicate, the more we know what's really happening and the more we can see where the threads of our tales come together. The more we discuss what is wrong, the more hope we have of finding solutions.

As a storyteller, I see layers of importance and empowerment in sharing our stories with each other. However, as a writer, I often tell my stories alone to my computer, and as an introvert with depressive tendencies, I often seek solitude. And I do need alone time to be my best—lots of it even. But since it's so comfortable, sometimes I stick to myself when I would get something great out of being with other people. Hanisch's essay reminds me that seeing friends and even interacting with people I don't know is a vital part of being human. A human apart has no energy to bounce off of, and even though I can always feel my battery ticking down when I'm around other people, sometimes I need to drain that battery to live fully.

In April 2016, I set off in a Winnebago motor home for a twenty-thousand-mile trip over eighteen months and through forty-four states. It's been completely amazing to see the range of geography that spans from the Atlantic to the Pacific, and the array of communities that have set roots in these places. I've explored some of the history that all but decimated the Native populations and that all but crushed the African populations that were brought here in chains, with the knowledge that so many more atrocities lay lost and forgotten in the dirt.

When the beast we call Trump was declared president-elect, I felt the call for community anew. I'm back in Oakland, California, building community

[168] MAUREEN JOHNSON

with friends and chosen family. The more interdependent we are, the more we are living the very lives conservatives fear us living: one filled with compassion and celebration, with love and with generosity, with dreams and possibilities galore. I want to share in joys and bear through sorrows together with my people. I aim to live my life in fierce defiance.

My guess is that most of you reading this don't live alone on the road in an RV. In fact, many of you live with parents and/or other adults who choose where you live, where you go to school, when you can be out, and lots more. Your family might not be affirming folks to talk with about what you see in the world. Your friends (or some of them) might not be either. That doesn't mean you shouldn't share what you think with them. But it does mean you deserve people to go to afterward, people whose beliefs you connect with, who respect you and who you respect. That doesn't mean you agree on everything, but you really do deserve a friendly ear.

Find your people and share in life with them. They might be from home, school, work, the internet, or elsewhere, but find them. And keep talking. Part of teenagehood is about feeling alone and different. Stay connected. You might even have meetings, like Hanisch and other feminists did, with the express purpose of sharing your stories. It might feel a little weird or fake, especially at first, but sometimes that layer of structure makes it easier to get people to drop some of their shields and join you in the scary world of honesty and openness. And that is where the fiercest and most powerful work to change the world is done: in connection.

If you can go there, you make it easier for other people to go there as well, and then suddenly you're deep in the messiness of reality together, living. And as you may have heard, living well is the best revenge. It's also The Resistance in action. Bring snacks to share!

Justin Mikita is a lawyer, producer, actor, and activist. After law school, he worked with the American Foundation for Equal Rights on marriage equality until it was achieved federally at the Supreme Court. He cofounded the social innovation firm Hawkins Mikita, which works with high-profile clients to develop philanthropic and activist strategies. Bridging the gap between entertainment and philanthropy, he highlights and affects change in a broad range of progressive issues. Follow him on Twitter and Instagram @JustinMikita.

Jesse Tyler Ferguson is an award-winning stage and screen actor who has performed on Broadway, in Shakespeare in the Park, and as the Emmy Award–nominated role of Mitchell Pritchett on the television show Modern Family. Jesse was named a celebrity ambassador for the ACLU in 2013. He and his husband, Justin Mikita, founded Tie The Knot, a nonprofit that sells curated designer products to raise money for organizations that champion LGBTQ rights worldwide. Follow him on Twitter and Instagram @JesseTyler.

What does "resistance" mean to you?

JUSTIN: Resistance means persistence. It means awareness and visibility.

JESSE: And being woke. As the kids say.

Where were you the first time you felt called to resist?

JUSTIN: In 2008 I was in my second year of law school. I was floundering, and wasn't very politically inclined. And then Prop 8 happened in California. [Note: Prop 8 was a California ballot proposition opposing same-sex marriage.] It was an eye-opening and appalling experience for me. Being the millennial I am, I just grew up expecting that even though I'm gay, I would grow up and get married. So when they took it from us, I felt so . . . activated in a way that I had never experienced. And it was my first time on the street with a banner in the rallies on Santa Monica Boulevard.

JESSE: When I was in high school in Albuquerque I was bullied pretty heavily. My defense mechanism was to stay quiet, keep my head down, get through the day. I would appreciate the people who just ignored me, for pretending I wasn't there.

[174] MAUREEN JOHNSON

My senior year I was obsessed with Tony Kushner's play *Angels in America*. [Note: *Angels in America: A Gay Fantasia on National Themes* is a two-part, Pulitzer-winning play from 1993 that explored AIDS and queerness in America in the 1980s.] I had read it many times. I was dying to see it in New York. And I decided to do a cutting of *Angels* for my high school speech and debate club—a very small group of four of us, at this sports-driven, Catholic high school.

Somehow, I won some awards for my performance, and was invited to go to the Bible Belt of Kansas City to do it at the national level. Before going, my English teacher asked me to do the monologue in front of class. I was the person who wanted to keep his head down, but I was like: I have something to say. So I'm going to resist in the way I know how: with my art.

It was terrifying. There were snickers from kids in the audience, once they realized what the material was about, and how homocentric it was. But I finished it. And the thing that surprised me is that the people who ignored me, and always passed by me, they said: You're really talented. You're going to be on Broadway someday. And I realized that by using your voice, even when it's scary, you bridge gaps.

And then I grew up and met Justin, and Tony Kushner married us.

Amazing story. I am struck by how much confidence and frankly how much access you guys have. What's something a young person today could do to start resisting?

JESSE: We have such access with social media, which didn't exist when I was a kid. So people are able to—with the good and the bad—form a voice.

They are able to reach out to people who are like-minded. I always encourage people to find like-minded people.

And I encourage people to get involved in the gay-straight alliance at their school. If they don't have one, ask for one. Being an activist earlier on doesn't necessarily mean standing on a soap box with a bullhorn. You figure out what's best for you and you do it your way.

JUSTIN: My big piece of advice is just visibility. Just being visible as an ally to every community, and there's a lot of them. We are all stronger together when we are actually fighting for each other. I challenge straight allies to celebrate pride month. Just like millions of people who don't identify as women went to the Women's March. You can do that at any level. Even locally, just supporting your local meetings or volunteering. All the way up to larger marches.

Where do you find hope, now?

JESSE: The good thing that's come out of the last few months is it's activated people. There's so much movement happening to better the country, from both sides. But it's hard to find a silver lining.

JUSTIN: I feel like I haven't stopped marching since 2008. I felt that way, honestly, through the bulk of Hillary's campaign, for which I was working hard, long before she even announced her candidacy. And marching. By the time the election came around, I felt so broken and sad. You know, all the things. When the Women's March showed up, I stayed home. I was like: I march every day, I'm going to sit this one out. But I'll never forget that day. That march. The amount of turnout. The images. I was flabbergasted; it was so beautiful.

[176] MAUREEN JOHNSON

Unfortunately, when given a lot of progress—like we were for eight years with Obama—we get complacent. There is a whole generation of new voters who have only ever known an Obama presidency. And all of that progress and dignity and acceptance and tolerance. So for some people, this is the first time they realize: we have to keep fighting. And by the way, we had to fight Obama for four years to come out for marriage. So what gives me hope is the beauty of the resistance. I've never seen people so active.

What's something you would tell your younger self about the future? Advice in general?

JESSE: I would tell myself to relax. I look back now at those people I'd never spoken to in high school, who came forward. You have to trust that there are people out there who are just as shy as you. And who are good people. And sometimes trusting mankind and trusting yourself is the first step to making a connection to someone.

Sabaa Tahir grew up in California's Mojave Desert at her family's eighteen-room motel. There, she spent her time devouring fantasy novels, raiding her brother's comic book stash, and playing guitar badly. She began writing An Ember in the Ashes while working nights as a newspaper editor. She likes thunderous indie rock, garish socks, and all things nerd. Sabaa currently lives in the San Francisco Bay Area. You can find her on Instagram, Twitter, and Tumblr @sabaatahir, and at www.SabaaTahir.com.

Resist with a kiss
in full sunshine
with the love who steals your heart.

Resist with your voice
"Call those reps, now!"
Shyness overcome by wrath.

Resist with silence
When they require
Vocal capitulation.

Resist with the flag
Red, white and blue
Mean freedom not oppression.

Resist with your words
Tell what you see
Spit truth when others dare not.

[180] MAUREEN JOHNSON

Resist with your hands
So that my children
Believe that good can still win.

Resist with rage
Resist with love
Resist with thought
Resist with votes
Resist with books
Resist with body
Resist with speech
Resist with heart
Resist.
Resist.
Resist.

Dana Schwartz is an arts and culture writer based in New York City who has been published by The New Yorker, The Guardian, The New York Observer, Marie Claire, Glamour, Mic, GQ, Vice, *and more. She's currently a correspondent at* Entertainment Weekly. *She created a parody Twitter account called* @GuyInYourMFA *based on the people she's encountered in fiction workshops, and another one called* @DystopianYA *about the tropes in all of the young adult fiction books she's read. Her own (nondystopian) YA book (*And We're Off*) was published May 2017 by Penguin/Razorbill, and a memoir (*Choose Your Own Disaster*) is forthcoming from Grand Central. Follow her on Instagram and Twitter* @DanaSchwartzzz.

THE JEWISH WE

Being Jewish felt like nothing, until it became something.

We grew up in the suburbs of Chicago, in a town where we felt bad for the kids who weren't Jewish. It somehow felt both like a club and the predominant culture: those of us who brought matzo in brown lunch bags during Passover exchanged smirks of recognition and traded our Passover-kosher desserts between ourselves (two flourless brownies for a bag of Passover cotton candy—of course, the local grocery store carried Passover cotton candy). Seventh grade was a whirlwind of weekly Bar and Bat Mitzvahs; we spent all of eighth grade wearing T-shirts that said things like "I had a BALL at Jason's Bar Mitzvah!" and sweatpants that declared "Becca's a Star!" across the butt. Maybe 60 percent of the kids in my town were Jewish, but it felt like 95 percent.

Since being Jewish was just an accepted trait about ourselves, we leaned into stereotypes and made jokes. "Ugh, you literally look like such a JAP right now," we said to the girls in Ugg boots, nursing a Starbucks cup. Being a Jewish American Princess was being basic before basic was a thing. "Jewish mothers, am I right?" we said, rolling our eyes as our phones lit up with half a dozen texts from a mother wondering whether we were staying longer at the mall or if she should come and pick us up. We said it. We told stories about friends of friends who met someone who had never met a Jew before. "Where are your horns?" that person had asked, the story goes, in

[184] MAUREEN JOHNSON

all earnestness. We told that story over and over until it became an urban legend, the type that could have been told around a campfire as the least scary scary story possible. We flatironed our curly brown hair straight and got nose jobs at sixteen and gossiped about who got nose jobs at sixteen and whether or not it turned out well. We dated boys in high school named David and Ari and Joshua. We asked our older sisters how to kiss boys. We were never afraid.

By college, we became aware that we had grown up in a tiny comfortable nest in a very big world—a world where most people didn't have closets overflowing with "I Danced the Night Away at Monica's Bat Mitzvah" sweatshirts. "It's not really a big deal," we'd say to people who asked about what it was like to be Jewish. "It's not ever really something I thought about. My family doesn't keep kosher or anything like that, just for Passover. And we only really go to temple on the holidays."

There were always comments online, inevitable, really—because comments online are always inevitable—"nice nose, Jew," "go die in an oven"—were laughable and quickly deleted, the desperate attempts at edgy humor by a fourteen-year-old in a basement somewhere, the same one who no doubt typed "go make me a sandwich!" as his next brilliant insult.

But then we saw the sea of people with red hats who shouted all sorts of things. Someone sent us a comment online telling us to go die in an oven, except this time it's our faces Photoshopped in the tiny window in the thick metal door, they took the time to find our pictures. And people like the photo, and comment below celebrating it. And all of the people keep celebrating each other, unashamed, and they have photos of Donald Trump as their Twitter avatars and when he wins they bellow, "WE HAVE DONE IT."

The messages kept coming. Lampshades. Faded yellow stars on skeletal corpses. Gas chambers. Train cars. Images meant to shock, and also to make us afraid.

They hate Muslims, they are allowed to be loud about that one, and they hate us, too—but for now, it's just a hatred most of them needed to keep anonymous and caged like a rabid animal, at least publicly. Photos of world leaders or lawyers with yellow stars plastered over them are passed around furtively on forums with an undying belief in a conspiracy theory that they know can't be shared in polite company.

It was a privilege—a tremendous, indulgent, coddling privilege—that we were able to develop believing Judaism to be an identifier of belonging, an aspect of identity that was both cool and celebrated in our small, upper-middle-class suburban bubble. It is a privilege that anti-Semitism is, for now, still considered taboo for the politicians in nice suits, at least compared to the public vitriol they can have toward Latinos and Muslims; a privilege too that publicly appearing as Jewish is something that can be disguised with a name-change and a blowout.

But hatred isn't something you only attempt to stem, like a flood, as soon as it makes your own hem wet. That hatred is loud and cruel and vicious for us, but it's louder and crueler and more vicious for so many others. We went through our adolescence wearing our Judaism proudly, but not too loudly, never too ostentatiously outside the bubble of our own town. There's something that's been sewn into our DNA after thousands of years of looking over our shoulders and leaving with what we could carry. Just be quiet, build a life for ourselves, they won't notice we're here, we're fine. And so we were quiet.

We were so lucky for so fucking long, but there is no excuse to be quiet about anything anymore.

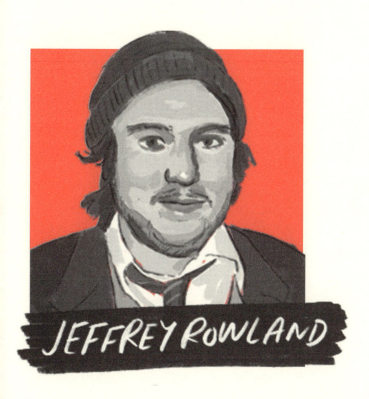

Jeffrey Rowland is a cartoonist and entrepreneur originally from Locust Grove, Oklahoma. One of webcomics' pioneers, he now runs TopatoCo.com, one of the world's leading online shops curating digital entertainment-related merchandise. He deftly escaped Oklahoma in the mid-2000s and now resides in a doomsday bunker in Northampton, Massachusetts.

KARUNA RIAZI

Karuna Riazi is a born and raised New Yorker with a loving, large extended family and the rather trying experience of being the eldest sibling in her particular clan. She holds a BA in English Literature from Hofstra University and is an online diversity advocate, blogger, and publishing intern, known for starting the viral #YesAllWomen hashtag. She is a 2017 honoree on NBC's Asian America's Redefining A–Z list, featuring up-and-coming talent within the Asian-American and Pacific Islander community, and her work has been featured in Entertainment Weekly, Amy Poehler's Smart Girls, Book Riot, and Teen Vogue, among others. The Gauntlet (S&S/Salaam Reads, 2017) is her first novel. Follow her on Twitter @KarunaRiazi.

REFILLING THE WELL

Recently, every word has been water wrenched from a stone.

Not merely squeezed. Not a quick heartbeat-clench around the firm, craggy surface, just enough to feel my spirits drop at the confirmation of mineral-reinforced stability, fingers to come away with a knowledge of chalky dust and weary, clumping age.

Every moment is a struggle, both hands holding firm, yielding whatever may come out to bead up whether it is sweat, or tears, or blood.

Many days, it feels like there is nothing left to my creativity except for a drought-dry crevice where it once flowed.

And this is how I resist, here and now. I keep the bucket in my hands. I keep the drops, the trickles, the small streams occasionally stumbled upon by kicked up rocks and frantic scrabbling, and I do what I can to refill my well.

For a good three years, I have deceived myself into believing my strength is bottomless. I have given again, and again, as I was expected to: as a woman, and a woman of color, and a woman of color in America, where you are always expected to have the advantage.

While being the one still standing while others have the seats.

While being the one holding your bleeding side while others withhold the bandages.

While being the one facing the slur—catching it in your hands like a flyaway ball, defining the raw scrape-ache coursing through your palm to the person who flung it at you, the person who now claims they do not know why that should hurt, why you wince, why your wrist hangs limp.

I pass on the bucket and I have been used to having it return empty, with holes stomped out in its bottom and moss clinging to its sides. I apologize for being tart, for being sharp, for being selfish and holding the handle of my bucket as I pass it down, pass my energy and voice and efforts on, for insisting that it is mine when others try to etch their names in it or grip it in their laps.

I have been emptied over the same movements that should, one day perhaps will, bring me pride. I have felt shame for the days when I am not facing forward and front and center, for the emails I have ignored because they asked for the dregs that would parch my own thirst, for the words that were needed to fill my own blank pages.

I have resolved to do better, to dip deeper.

It would not run out.

Now, I stand here and I clench my fingers around a stone, and I look down into the well and see the faint glimmers of potential and rippling, quenching promise at its very bottom.

And I resolve to resist.

It may sound selfish. It may feel selfish. I've been berated, as the creator of a viral movement that was based on the premise of women's unity, on the days when I dig in my heels, brace myself, and focus on tugging up that bucket for myself—in utter silence and solitude, or with the intention of sharing what I find within myself, or without, with a certain few. There is so much in me that has been geared to pamper, to please, to make myself palatable and likeable and have the right words to offer forward in my clasped hands without any of the eloquence or education or God knows whatever else I must willingly give slipping through the cracks in my fingers.

To go against that desire, for instance, as a Muslim woman, to stand up and act as a representative of the true narrative—to carry an entire religion's decisions, interpretations, dialogues, and discussions on my shoulders at all given times—often feels like it goes against my entire purpose of being.

But it is not my purpose of being. It is not the reason why I have this well to draw from. There is no reason that my words, as I use them, as I spend them or replenish them, are immediately slotted to be used for someone else, to enlighten someone else, to defend someone else, to engage someone else.

And it does not mean I do not share what is in me to give. It does not mean that refilling my well requires a lack of interaction, interchanging of ideas, or hands stretched outward.

This is how I resist, here and now: I keep the bucket in my hands. I fill it with hopeful sunrises, the smiles and strength of my students who must resist this world and the way it drains us and freely dribbles away what we have to offer it, the peace of prostration in prayer, moments when I do feel the right words or the stream of consciousness rolling and bounding and funneling back into its rightful place.

My strength is not bottomless.

My grief, my defeat, my days of deep darkness—the days in which we all cannot help but be tethered to the headlines, helpless and hindered by all we want to do and should do and yet cannot begin to fix—do not define me, but they are also not meant to be struggled through with a dry mouth and eyes and an empty well.

This is how I do better and dig deeper. This is how I continue to live, and brace myself for the occasional ball I cannot help but catch, and have enough left to give in the best ways I can possibly give.

I keep the bucket in my hands and I refill my well.

THE BIGNESS TRAP

So, here we are at the end of the book. I hope you got something out of this, something to inspire you, something that makes you want to get active!

Perhaps you are also thinking: BUT THE PROBLEMS ARE SO BIG AND I AM BUT ONE PERSON HOW AM I SUPPOSED TO FIX ALL THIS STUFF?

Ah. The BIGNESS TRAP. When things seem too big, we think we can't accomplish them and we do nothing. I have good news: you do not have to fix the world alone. No one fixes the world alone. Bit by bit, we work together, and we make change. Don't let the bigness of the problem fool you. All problems can be knocked down to size if we all get out there and take a whack at them.

So go write your post, or sing your song, or make your machine, or build a site, or talk to that person, or go to that march, or read that book, or, or, or . . .

This part is up to you. The possibilities are genuinely endless, and you can do as much or as little as you want, in any combination, at any time.

I do have some final tips, if you want them.

Don't let anyone steal your joy: After the election of 2016, I said this a lot, when it became clear that Trump was going to be president and the color seemed to seep out of the world. I said, "Don't let Trump steal your joy." You can substitute whatever you need to for the word Trump. There

[198] MAUREEN JOHNSON

will always be something that casts a shadow. Remember, what's yours is yours—your music, your words, your books, your loves. Hang on to them and take care of them.

Read widely and often: It's one of the best defenses against totalitarianism.

Don't be afraid of failure: Failure is your buddy. You usually have to fail at making something before you finish making something, so consider failing to be a critical step and high-five yourself for it.

Never, ever give up.

THE BEGINNER'S GUIDE TO BOOKS ON RESISTANCE

When I got the idea to include a "starter library" of resistance books for teens, I realized there'd be nobody better to ask than librarians (aka superheroes). I put out a request for librarians' favorite titles on Twitter and got hundreds of responses; here are the books on action and activism that came up again and again:

1984 by George Orwell—from Renee in Minnesota

A Is for Activist by Innosanto Nagara—from Allison in Illinois

All the Rage by Courtney Summers—from Mars in Wisconsin

Be a Changemaker: How to Start Something That Matters by Laurie Ann Thompson—from Danielle in Washington

Between the World and Me by Ta-Nehisi Coates—from Faythe in California

Claudette Colvin: Twice Toward Justice by Phillip M. Hoose—from Catherine in New York

[200] THE BEGINNER'S GUIDE TO BOOKS ON RESISTANCE

Dear Martin by Nic Stone—from Kat in New York

The Disreputable History of Frankie Landau-Banks by E. Lockhart—from Cameron in Maine

Flesh & Blood So Cheap: The Triangle Fire and Its Legacy by Albert Marrin—from Jane in Kentucky

Girl Rising: Changing the World One Girl at a Time by Tanya Lee Stone—from Amanda in New Jersey

The Handmaid's Tale by Margaret Atwood—from Elizabeth in New York

The Hate U Give by Angie Thomas—from Sarah in New Brunswick

I Am Malala: How One Girl Stood Up for Education and Changed the World by Malala Yousafzai with Patricia McCormick—from Kate in North Carolina

I Dissent: Ruth Bader Ginsburg Makes Her Mark by Debbie Levy—from Mary in Colorado

Long Walk to Freedom by Nelson Mandela—from Melissa in Ohio

Loving vs. Virginia: A Documentary Novel of the Landmark Civil Rights Case by Patricia Hruby Powell—from Pam in Massachusetts

March: Books 1–3 by John Lewis—from Jez in Illinois

THE BEGINNER'S GUIDE TO BOOKS ON RESISTANCE [201]

On Tyranny: Twenty Lessons from the Twentieth Century by Timothy Snyder—from Joe in Ohio

Pride: The Story of Harvey Milk & the Rainbow Flag by Rob Sanders—from Ellie in Maryland

Sit-In: How Four Friends Stood Up by Sitting Down by Andrea Davis Pinkney—from Laura in Indiana

Stonewall: Breaking Out in the Fight for Gay Rights by Ann Bausum—from Jill in Ohio

We Should All Be Feminists by Chimamanda Ngozi Adichie—from Laurie in Oregon

We've Got a Job: The 1963 Birmingham Children's March by Cynthia Levinson—from Brittany in Illinois